Darkest Secrets of Spiritual Seduction Masters:

How to Protect Yourself,
Boost Your Psychological Immune System
and Strengthen Your Spirit

Tom Marcoux

America's Communication Coach
Speaker-Author of 22 books
Blogger, BeHeardandBeTrusted.com
Comparative Religion Instructor, college level

A QuickBreakthrough Publishing Edition

Copyright © 2014, 2011 Tom Marcoux Media, LLC
ISBN: 0615947484
ISBN-13: 978-0615947488

All rights reserved. No part of this book may be reproduced or transmitted in any form by any means electronic or mechanical, including photocopying, recording or by any information storage and retrieval system without written permission from the publisher.

QuickBreakthrough Publishing is an imprint of Tom Marcoux Media, LLC. More copies are available from the publisher, Tom Marcoux Media, LLC. Write TomSuperCoach@gmail.com

or visit www.TomSuperCoach.com

or Tom's blog: www.BeHeardandBeTrusted.com

This book was developed and written with care. Names and details were modified to respect privacy.

Disclaimer: The author and publisher acknowledge that each person's situation is unique, and that readers have full responsibility to seek consultations with health, financial, spiritual and legal professionals. The author and publisher make no representations or warranties of any kind, and the author and publisher shall not be liable for any special, consequential or exemplary damages resulting, in whole or in part, from the reader's use of, or reliance upon, this material.:

Other Books by Tom Marcoux:
- Be Heard and Be Trusted: How to Get What You Want
- Nothing Can Stop You This Year!
- Darkest Secrets of Persuasion and Seduction Masters
- Darkest Secrets of Charisma
- Darkest Secrets of Negotiation Masters
- Darkest Secrets of the Film and Television Industry Every Actor Should Know
- Darkest Secrets of Making a Pitch to the Film and Television Industry
- Darkest Secrets of Film Directing
- Darkest Secrets of Small Business Marketing

Praise for *Darkest Secrets of Spiritual Seduction Masters*:

"This book will save lives and also help people connect with a nourishing spirituality." – Dr. JoAnn Dahlkoetter, author of *Your Performing Edge*, Coach to CEOs and Olympic Gold Medalists

"This book points out the tricks of [certain] malevolent people and how to avoid them. The techniques in this book can help strengthen you and guide you on how to protect those you love. Tom Marcoux knows what he is talking about. A close friend of his committed suicide . . . Now Marcoux seeks to prevent other such tragedies. You can learn a lot from his book." – Danek S. Kaus, author of *You Can Be Famous: Insider Secrets to Getting Free Publicity*

Praise for Tom Marcoux's Other Work

"*Create Your Best Life* is an uplifting and practical book. You'll learn skills in persuasion, charisma, confidence, influence and emotional strength — all vital elements to help you positively change the world. To make a dream come true, you'll need to get people enrolled in your vision. This is *the book* that helps you get great things done!" – Dr. JoAnn Dahlkoetter, author of *Your Performing Edge* and coach to CEOs and Olympic Gold Medalists

"In *Darkest Secrets of Persuasion and Seduction Masters*, learn useful countermeasures to protect you from being darkly manipulated."
– David Barron, co-author, *Power Persuasion*

"In *Be Heard and Be Trusted*, Tom's advice on how to remain true to yourself and establish authentic rapport with clients is both insightful and reality based. He [shows how] to establish oneself as a credible expert." -Arthur P. Ciaramicoli, Ed.D., Ph.D., author *The Curse of the Capable*, and *The Power of Empathy*

"*Nothing Can Stop You This Year* is a treasure trove of tips, tools, and terrific ideas—practical, reassuring, and energizing! Tom provides wonderful resources for achieving your goals." – Elayne Savage, Ph.D., author of *Don't Take It Personally! The Art of Dealing with Rejection*

Visit Tom's blog: www.BeHeardandBeTrusted.com

Tom Marcoux

CONTENTS

Dedication and Acknowledgments	i
A. Book One: 10 Vulnerabilities to Spiritual Seduction (and Your Countermeasures)	7
B. Book Two: Darkest Secrets of Spiritual Seduction Masters (Dark Seducer's Methods and Your Countermeasures)	85
C. Book Three: How to Strengthen Your Spirit (Tune into Your Divine Gifts)	141
D. Book Four. How to Strengthen Your Spirit (The 10 Topics)	181
A Final Word and Springboard to Your Dreams	225
Excerpt from *Darkest Secrets of Persuasion and Seduction Masters: How to Protect Yourself and Turn the Power to Good* by Tom Marcoux	227
About the Author Tom Marcoux	240
Special Offer Just for Readers of this Book	242

DEDICATION AND ACKNOWLEDGEMENTS

This book is dedicated to "Joe." We miss you.
Many blessings to you.
Special thanks to the team that made this book possible. Thanks to the terrific author and book/film consultant, Johanna E. Mac Leod for terrific insights. It is also dedicated to the other team members. Thanks to Linda L. Chappo, David MacDowell Blue, and Joan Harrison for editing. Also, thanks to two more colleagues (who requested anonymity), one who did some editing and another who did the cover photography and rendering of the front cover. Thanks to my father, Al Marcoux, for his concern and efforts for me. Thanks to my mother, Sumiyo Marcoux, a kind, generous soul. Thanks to Johanna E. Mac Leod for rendering the back cover. Thank you to Higher Power. Thanks to our readers, audiences, clients, my graduate/college students and my team members of Tom Marcoux Media, LLC.

BOOK ONE:
10 VULNERABILITIES TO SPIRITUAL SEDUCTION
(AND YOUR COUNTERMEASURES)

I never thought I'd write a book like this. But then something happened that broke my heart. My dear friend killed himself. Joe* died with an open religious book next to him. That's how Joe was found, in his car with a gun in the glove compartment. He didn't need the firearm; the pills had accomplished his purpose.

To help you protect yourself from manipulation, I'm going to alert you to what I call the *10 Vulnerabilities to Spiritual Seduction*. Joe had suffered from seven of these 10 Vulnerabilities. And he's dead now.

Thinking of Joe now, I feel tears in my eyes. I remember his laughter and his sense of humor. He was not a prude, but he'd put his fingers into his ears, saying "La, la, la, too much information!" And what a good listener Joe was. You could see it in his eyes. He was completely present with you. So much compassion.

---

* "Joe" is a pseudonym to spare his family and friends further pain.

I could not save Joe. But through this book, I can be your coach so that you can strengthen yourself. You'll learn to empower yourself to face many uncomfortable or threatening situations.

It's helpful that you know that I myself have a spiritual path. This book appreciates religion. In fact, I have taught Comparative Religion on the college level for over 12 years. In my class, students talk about the benefits they see arising from various religions.

We all walk through life with vulnerabilities. Along the way, we stumble now and then. At times, we lose our balance. Some of us fall. But some of us are pushed. Or tripped. Or led blindfolded to the edge of a cliff and abandoned. In hindsight—too late—I see how that happened with Joe. No, not with him. To him. Someone did that to my friend. The book in your hand now shows what I learned in the wake of that tragedy. It is a warning. More, it is a guide.

Earlier I said "strengthen yourself," and that's the process of developing empowering patterns of thoughts and behaviors. I have survived serious vehicle accidents that sent me to the hospital. So I know that bad things happen. We need to be strong to withstand the storms of life.

In my Comparative Religion class, I function as a reporter sharing various ideas, and I'll do that here through quotes drawn from wisdom of various cultures—and scientific research. So we'll have the opportunity to look at spiritual paths from a number of perspectives, which provide more choices for you to approach life in an empowered manner.

The subtitle of this book advises: "Boost Your Psychological Immune System."

Renowned Harvard psychologist Daniel Gilbert wrote in his book *Stumbling on Happiness*, "... a *psychological immune system* . . . defends the mind against unhappiness in much the same way that the physical immune system defends the body against illness." The phrase *psychological immune system* captured my attention. And I thought of providing *countermeasures* here which can function as your "antibodies."

10 Vulnerabilities to Spiritual Seduction

The Vulnerabilities about which I wrote earlier are most easily explained in terms of the following questions. For simplicity's sake, the questions use the form of asking "you." But they work just as well when asked about someone else. Remember, we all have some vulnerabilities:

1) Do you experience low self-esteem?
2) Do you feel guilty a lot?
3) Are you overly impressed by titles?
4) Do you actively long for friends?
5) Do you consider your appearance "below average"?
6) Do you still suffer from the end of a relationship?
7) Does your sexual orientation upset you?
8) Do you feel a lack of hope or aliveness?
9) Do you experience any form of mental illness?
10) Do you feel you can't get a good night's sleep?

The editors of this book suggested replacing the above questions with statements. I kept them because they invite us to offer answers.

Now let's look at each question. I'll provide Countermeasures for each topic.

Tom Marcoux

VULNERABILITY #1: DO YOU EXPERIENCE LOW SELF-ESTEEM?
(10 Vulnerabilities to Spiritual Seduction)

Joe experienced low self-esteem and it made him vulnerable to depression.

Many of us have heard that having high self-esteem is helpful to enjoying life and achieving what we want. But we rarely hear or read a definition. What is self-esteem?

One definition from author and psychologist Nathaniel Branden includes:

"Self-esteem is the disposition to experience oneself as being competent to cope with the basic challenges of life and of being worthy of happiness. It is confidence in the efficacy of our mind, in our ability to think. By extension, it is confidence in our ability to learn, make appropriate choices and decisions, and respond effectively to change. It is also the experience that success, achievement, fulfillment—happiness—are right and natural for us."

We can think of self-esteem as "fuel." Without fuel, the

car cannot get us to a neighboring city.

Some people mistakenly look upon self-esteem as some form of self-obsession. Certain individuals say, "She likes herself too much" or "That guy is always talking about himself." This is not about self-esteem.

Instead, *self-esteem is the belief in our capacity to do well in life.*

On the other hand, there are individuals who want you to have low self-esteem . . .

The Manipulators Who Want You to Have Low Self-Esteem are the "Opportunists" and "Guilters"

Who are the people who seek to push you around when it comes to spiritual matters? I provide two different labels, to distinguish between two sets of motivations:

• **Opportunists (or "insincere opportunists"):** These people do not believe in spirituality, in religion, or even in any kind of faith. They merely use the language of a church or religious movement to manipulate people and to pluck money from many people's wallets. Some go further. A certain percentage become sexual predators. But whether after money or flesh, or both, Opportunists look at us and do not see people. Instead, they see targets.

• **Guilters:** Some devout people subscribe to the idea that "it is important that everyone feel guilty and terrible—and to live in mortal terror of punishment." They genuinely believe each human being needs to be torn down to nothing–and then, the person must rely on the Guilter for some kind of "rules." The Guilter claims that he or she is the go-between for the listener and Higher Power. The Guilter insists no one can ever feel inner peace unless abiding by "the rules."

[I will leave it to you, the reader, to decide which category may apply to an individual. Soon I'll discuss another category "Spiritual Leaders."]

Opportunists and Guilters Perpetrate Spiritual Seduction

What is Spiritual Seduction?

Spiritual Seduction, as opposed to enlightenment or teaching, shows certain signs. Their presence pretty much defines what this term means:

a) **False Promises**—aimed at fostering disloyalty to one's own self, in other words we are tempted to betray ourselves in return for some fabulous rewards (which remain invisible).

b) **Emotional Sticks and Carrots**—in other words, the seducer makes a person feel terrible, alone and hopeless and then offers relief.

c) **Assumed Authority**—someone claims the position of personal ambassador or liaison between the listener and a Higher Power.

d) **Obedience Before All**—the seducer teaches no one can ever feel inner peace except by following rules–rules the seducer of course provides but may not be questioned.

e) **Divine Terror**—fostering an abiding vision of a Higher Power who can, will and does punish the guilty.

f) **Compassion Despised**—vitally, spiritual seduction requires its targets not feel compassion, not only for others but especially not for themselves.

The elimination of compassion leads to cruel behavior.

Belief in a cruel God makes a cruel man. —Thomas Paine

Why do people engage in Spiritual Seduction? It is about controlling other people.

What is the Opposite of Spiritual Seduction?

Nourishment of the Soul is the opposite of Spiritual Seduction.

What does such nourishment do for you? It inspires you to fulfill your potential. You feel comforted and empowered to have a productive and enjoyable life. When I say nourishment, I also mean "spiritual nourishment."

Some might talk about enlightenment or spiritual awakening. And I'll include those topics under the umbrella of Nourishment of the Soul.

Spiritual Leaders Provide Nourishment of the Soul

What do *Spiritual Leaders* do? They provide inspiration and encouragement. They light the way to higher levels of human functioning that includes compassion, courage, loyalty, faith, grace and love. Spiritual Leaders demonstrate compassion. A classic definition of compassion is *"Deep awareness of the suffering of another coupled with the wish to relieve it."* (thefreedictionary.com)

Some spiritual leaders demonstrate compassion throughout their adult years.

At other times, we may find nourishment in the words of someone who may have been momentarily gifted with a nourishing idea. *I leave it to you, the reader, to decide if someone* is truly a spiritual leader or just a conduit of an empowering idea at a given moment.

Here are some helpful ideas:

Take the first step in faith. You don't have to see the whole staircase, just take the first step. —Martin Luther King, Jr.

You must be the change you wish to see in the world. —Mahatma Gandhi

Believe nothing, no matter where you read it, or who said it, no matter if I have said it, unless it agrees with your own reason and your own common sense. —Buddha

Love your neighbor as yourself. —Jesus, the Christ

This last quote reminds me that we must be kind to ourselves so that we have the capacity to be kind to others.

If you want others to be happy, practice compassion. If you want to be happy, practice compassion. —The Dalai Lama

Be gentle first with yourself—if you wish to be gentle with others. —Lama Yeshe

Let's return to defining Spiritual Seduction:

The Merriam-Webster Dictionary defines *seduce* as "to persuade to disobedience or disloyalty . . . and to lead astray usually by persuasion or false promises." What "disloyalty"? We're talking about disloyalty to that which is already good inside you. If an Opportunist or Guilter makes you feel like you're a piece of garbage, you can become disloyal to yourself and fail to be compassionate towards yourself. This lack of compassion not only makes you miserable, but such misery spreads to people near you. Unhappy people often express anger and bitterness. It's a spreading poison in our homes and workplaces.

The Merriam-Webster Dictionary defines *spiritual* as "of, relating to, consisting of, or affecting the spirit: incorporeal . . . 2) of or relating to sacred matters . . . 3) concerned with religious values . . . 4) related or joined in spirit . . . 5) of or relating to supernatural beings or phenomena."

How does spiritual seduction occur? First, you are a spiritual being.

We are not human beings having a spiritual experience. We are spiritual beings having a human experience. —Pierre Teilhard de Chardin

So spiritual seduction twists a human being toward feeling guilty and worthless. And the vile spiritual seduction pulls a human being away from his or her essence as a benevolent and positive part of this universe. Therefore, spiritual seduction is an evil activity.

All that is necessary for the triumph of evil is that good men do nothing. —Edmund Burke

The first thing to do to protect yourself from spiritual seduction is to guard your self-esteem. Here's the secret: the person with good self-esteem will "stay in the game." He or she will persist. This person will keep going when all others give up. Why? Because the person with good self-esteem knows that he or she can adapt to whatever comes up in life. The pessimistic person is more likely to give up.

What happens when spiritual seduction creates pessimism and drains people's energy? The world loses innovative solutions, creative works and simply positive people who could uplift the moods of those around them.

Recently, a pessimistic friend of mine said, "I don't daydream." I felt a stab of pain for my friend. Why? Because he cannot see "more and better." Without any vision, he does not take small actions that can lead to more joy, success and fulfillment. He remains stuck.

Why does an Opportunist or Guilter want to lower people's self-esteem? First, it provides the Opportunist or Guilter with a purpose. If the Opportunist or Guilter convinces people that they are "broken and in exile," then the Opportunist or Guilter becomes the "keeper of the rules and answers" and the path to feel better.

Where do people hear about these rules? At a church service, for example. Some of my friends mention that they have felt peaceful during a church service. Others say that they feel that a service is just one of *many ways* to experience inner peace.

Often, an Opportunist or Guilter will claim that his or her church service (or Sunday meeting) is the *only way (or best way)* to gain access to God. Be careful when you hear someone say that there is only one way. Allowing someone to restrict your point of view can negatively impact your self-esteem. Why? Because you're allowing someone to dictate what is "good" and what is "wrong."

One of the things that blocks our efforts to learn about the world and the people in it is the nature of the stories we are told, come to believe, and tell others about how things work. This shared mythology, if it is incorrect, interferes with our efforts to understand ourselves and others and ultimately leads to bad decisions in the same way as explorers attempting to find their way with inadequate maps. —Gordon Livingston, M.D.

One important way to maintain high self-esteem is to gain access to multiple points of view and create a life of constant learning from a variety of sources.

Isn't high self-esteem a problem? Some people who focus on spiritual matters are concerned about an excessive focus on self-esteem. This can come from a confusion about a true *difference* between self-love and selfishness. Pastor and author Duke Robinson wrote about the confusion between self-love versus selfishness: "To be selfish is to be so preoccupied with ourselves that we are unable to consider the rights and needs of others. . . . In contrast . . . self-love calls us to the delicate balance of loving others at the same time, in the same ways, and to the same extent that we love ourselves."

Let's look at the contrasting details of self-love versus selfishness.

Self-Love
- Healthy focus on creating your capacity to get things done
- Healthy attitude about who you are and your place in the universe—"not below and not above other people"
- Treating yourself kindly like a valued friend.

Selfishness
- Excessive focusing on yourself
- Designating yourself as better and more important than other people
- Pretending that you feel that you're better than others

when you are harboring severe self-doubt

So let's return to the question: "Is high self-esteem a problem?" No. But selfishness can be a problem.

As children, we take in messages about selfishness. In addition, we hear messages like "Don't fool yourself. You're not that smart." Such a message causes trouble in a number of ways. But it does remind us of a different problem: *self-delusion*. Researchers have noted how some individuals delude themselves in their estimates of how skillful they are—or whether they have adequate and accurate knowledge. The solution for this is humility. Humility has two important parts: to be open to input and to perceive that one can have an incomplete perception in the moment. When we're humble we realize that we don't see the whole picture, and we are open to learning new ideas. Some people call this being coachable. A player who is coachable will take in guidance from the coach and she will improve her techniques and up the level of her game.

Humility and self-esteem are *not* mutually exclusive. In fact, they go hand-in-hand in helping you experience success and fulfillment. Any time you succeed at something also retain a focus on being coachable. Why? Self-esteem is a belief in your capacity to adapt and to make the most of your current opportunities. To truly know that you can adapt, you need to realize that you will be humble to learn from every experience. You can practice humility by realizing that you may not be seeing all of the vital components of a situation. With appropriate humility, you can then seek guidance and improve your methods in life. One of my editors asked, "Can't people without humility seek guidance?" Yes. But it takes humility to allow yourself to be influenced by benevolent guidance.

We see this all the time with top athletes relying on coaches to better their game.

Here are Countermeasures against someone trying to lower your self-esteem:

a) Become "spiritually strong"

The antidote for negative spiritual seduction is for you to become spiritually strong.

This antidote also helps you raise your self-esteem.

First, we need to connect with your motivation to become spiritually strong. Why would you want to be strong anyway? Perhaps you want to reduce pain in your life. Or you want to be nobody's fool. One way to say this is: "I don't want to be a victim ever again."

Many people find their motivation through a realization connected to this question: Who do you love? I realize that a number of people trudge through life without close friendships and loving interactions. For example, I know someone, "Sam," who said, "All I care about is whether I have a good workout and that I make progress with lifting weights." Now if this is Sam's way to happiness, that's fine. However, Sam is one of the most miserable people I have met. Why? Things go wrong with his workout. He gets injured or catches a cold. His workout fails to yield gains in strength and he told me that makes his whole day "bad." His whole day? Meanwhile, he lives alone, talks with few people and says he has no best friend.

What if Sam had multiple ways to be happy? Perhaps Sam may benefit from the old phrase "Happiness is something to do, someone to love and something to hope for." To bring more facets to one's life can create more opportunities for expressing love and feeling fulfilled.

A life lived merely for the self can be barren. My point is: when we seek to be strong for someone we love, we often have a powerful motivation on a whole new level.

Being deeply loved by someone gives you strength; loving someone deeply gives you courage. —Lao-Tzu

In my book Nothing Can Stop You This Year, I wrote about the "for-the-team" person. Some people will do more for their children (for example) than for themselves. I remember a friend told me that she brought her young daughter to her band rehearsals. She said, "I was teaching my daughter to go for her dreams." My friend told me that she had to muster extra strength to work a regular job and pursue music because she wanted to be a positive role model for her daughter. This is an example of stretching oneself due to loving another person.

So some readers of this book may be more motivated to complete reading this book and practice the methods so that they can be strong and *present* for their loved ones. I deeply support that.

The block of granite which is an obstacle in the pathway of the weak, becomes a stepping-stone in the pathway of the strong.
—Thomas Carlyle

This book helps you to be spiritually strong. How? You will become aware of the *10 Vulnerabilities to Spiritual Seduction* and you learn *countermeasures* against the dark tactics of Opportunists and Guilters.

When you assert yourself as an individual, choosing your

own beliefs and what you do with your discretionary time, you are likely to encounter resistance from people around you.

Great spirits have always encountered violent opposition from mediocre minds. –Albert Einstein

When you find your own heartfelt values, you will probably encounter opposition. Let's say that a group of friends expects you to simply follow their preferences and even their beliefs. When you go your own way, you will probably encounter criticism. For example, Molly enjoyed Celtic dancing on Wednesdays. Her new set of "religious friends" said, "Dancing? Don't you remember that we have [religious book] study on Wednesday? Dancing is frivolous. Your spirit is more important. You're going to be at the study group, right?"

Upon reflection, Molly realized that Celtic dancing was good for her physical health and it raised her mood every week. She looked forward to dancing all week long. This quote appealed to her:

Do what you feel in your heart to be right—for you'll be criticized anyway.—Eleanor Roosevelt

When I talk about being "spiritually strong," I include Eleanor's idea of "what you feel in your heart to be right (for you)." To be your own person, to go your own way, requires you to be courageous.

*Life shrinks or expands in proportion to one's courage.
—Anais Nin*

It takes courage to face the 10 Vulnerabilities and to devote effort to study how you can be strong. I applaud that you're reading this book. Good for you!

To study and practice the methods of becoming strong, you embark on a new journey.

It takes a lot of courage to release the familiar and seemingly secure in order to embrace the new and unknown. — Alan Cohen

Each day, I consider this useful question: "Does this strengthen me?" I submit my beliefs to this question. I also submit my actions. When you study this book and practice the countermeasures, naturally you strengthen yourself. How? It is like exercising muscles you didn't know you had. In addition, later in this book, we'll take your strength to another level as we discuss connecting with your Divine Gifts.

My friend Joe, who committed suicide, was not feeling strong and did not have full access to his Divine Gifts. (I didn't realize this until later as I put some pieces together while talking with his friends and family members.) I decided to do research into suicide and other topics for this book. I learned of Dr. Edward M. Hallowell's work that has saved Harvard Chemistry Department students from committing suicide. In his book, *Shine: Using Brain Science to Get the Best From Your People,* Dr. Hallowell wrote:

"It turned out this most recent suicide was just one in a long string of suicides going back for years in the department. The culture of the department left students desperate and isolated. [Responding to my suggestions, the chair of the department] Jim Anderson made changes in the department . . . He brought students together for biweekly buffets in the department library. The shy, socially awkward chemistry grad students and postdocs who would never come out for a mixer could be enticed to come out for food! Jim changed the advising system so that students had more than one professor to turn to in case a relationship soured. He even changed the architecture of the building, replacing heavy oak doors with glass, and adding a piano and espresso bar where canisters of chemicals used to be stored. He convened a quality-of-life committee that he actually listened to and he enacted many of their suggestions. Gradually the culture of cynicism, pessimism, and disconnection gave way to a culture of connection. [Over the recent ten years], there have been no suicides."

Think about it. How are you running your life? Do you have a personal "culture of cynicism, pessimism and disconnection"? If so, then you are not strengthening yourself. In fact, as noted in Dr. Hallowell's above experiences, a person may fall vulnerable to suicidal tendencies.

But this is NOT for you. You can take personal action, as outlined in this book, to strengthen yourself.

It takes courage to grow up and turn out to be who you really are. —*E. E. Cummings*

One man with courage makes a majority. — *Andrew Jackson*

As you look at the above quotes, I invite you to refer again to this question: "Does this strengthen me?"

Look at the messages that Opportunists and Guilters are attempting to press on you. Peer closely at your own beliefs, and ask, "Does this strengthen me?"

Remember, an Opportunist is someone who does not believe in a spiritual path and merely uses religious talk to manipulate others for personal gain. And recall that a Guilter is a devout person who holds to the idea that people must feel guilty and terrible and fear punishment from Higher Power. The Guilter often places himself as the go-between from Higher Power to the listener.

An unintelligent use of mind can only produce an unintelligent result. —Raymond Charles Barker

To let someone else tell you what to believe can result in an unintelligent use of your mind. In fact, you could make yourself vulnerable to manipulation at the hands of an Opportunist or Guilter.

I'm dedicated to the intelligent use of the mind. As a college instructor of Comparative Religion, I guide my students to view the benefits that many people across the world derive from their spiritual path. Related to that, in a later section, we'll explore a non-denominational spiritual discussion of love, forgiveness, humility, faith, grace and art—that I call Divine Gifts.

b) Treat yourself like you treat a cherished friend.

Do you criticize and tear down your good friend? Probably, you are kind to your friend. So why allow the opposite—letting some Opportunist or Guilter to tear you down? Imagine this: treat yourself like you would treat a cherished friend. What happens? You feel better; you have more energy. You're getting the nurturing you need. And you treat people around you in better ways. That's a great service to us all.

c) Start keeping promises to yourself

Some authors including Brian Tracy and Zig Ziglar noted that it's tough to feel good about yourself if you set a goal and don't take action to fulfill it. One solution is to start small. If you want to expand your mind by reading, give yourself a small goal of reading two pages a day, and then fulfill that goal!

Here's an important promise to keep to yourself: "I promise to limit my exposure to Opportunists and Guilters."

This is in line with the observations of Dr. Stan Kapuchinski, a board-certified psychiatrist and assistant professor of psychiatry at the University of Connecticut. Dr. Kapuchinski describes passive-aggressive behavior. He says that a person exhibiting passive-aggressive personality disorder ("PA") "traps you in situations in which everything you do or say is wrong" and "a PA controls you with guilt."

Dr. Kapuchinski writes that PAs "maintain the self-image of being a forlorn victim of life." He continues, "You think that being a good and helpful person will help PAs. You will not save them. You will never make them happy. You will only be miserable."

I'm including Dr. Kapuchinski's comments here for two reasons:

1) *Some of us have a facet of ourselves that functions like a PA.* (It would help if we start paying attention and to shift our habitual thoughts. At times, habitual thoughts can act like prison bars holding us back.)

2) *Some of us are reacting to the Guilters as if they are PAs.* (As noted above, a PA traps you in situations in which everything you do or say is wrong. Have your noticed how angry or bitter some atheist standup comedians (like George Carlin) come across? It appears that they are reacting to

restrictions and stress they found in some forms of organized religion that was pressed on them. What's the solution? You can limit your exposure to Guilters.

When you want to enjoy high levels of positive energy, limit your exposure to negative influences. For example, Robert often listened to songs, during high school, from a particular horror movie's soundtrack. The songs were bitter and promoted a dark view of life—just a perfect match for a rebellious teenager's point of view. Recently, Robert saw the music album available on Amazon.com. He noted that it was now twenty years later. Since his teenage years, Robert has found his way in the world with a family he loves. He is grateful for the blessings in his life. And *he made a deliberate decision to avoid buying* that music album. Each day, he continues to choose a different path.

Robert, by avoiding the old songs, is shifting his thought patterns. How? He is allowing certain neural connections to lose their strength. Clusters of brain cells (neurons) become accustomed to "firing together." So Robert's avoidance of the old songs ensures that certain neural connections fade through disuse. Robert avoided listening to the old, negative songs and thereby he let fade those old patterns of thoughts and feelings.

Similarly, if you have a Guilter in your life, you may choose to avoid that person or at least decrease your exposure time.

d) Use your brain to help you get stronger.

Due to tough circumstances that I have endured, including physically defending myself from multiple attackers and even my own father, I resolved over thirty years ago to strengthen myself. I practice martial arts kicks and palm strikes everyday. I study every day, reading up to

85 books in one year. I have taught people how to protect their lives as I gave them lessons in swimming and karate. And I continue to teach communication skills for positive results.

In my studies about how the brain operates, I noted that practice, training and rehearsal are vital to improving our skills and to gain the results we want. Researcher Raoul Oudejan of the MOVE Research Institute at Vrije University in Amsterdam conducted studies that demonstrated that *practicing under mild levels of stress can prevent one from choking when high levels of stress occur.*

This is an important insight. And this is related to how this book can help you. In order to train effectively, you need to know your vulnerable points and to learn countermeasures to the tactics of Opportunists and Guilters.

e) Develop friendships in which you can be yourself.

It helps to have multiple friends. Why? Because I've noticed that I can share different parts of my true self to varying degrees with different friends.

For example, as a writer, I like to give credit for other writers' excellent phrases. However, I have a friend who has a pet peeve about my using quotes as I describe my thoughts about a topic. So I modify how I speak in her presence. I'm not interested in the needless causing of disharmony. And I certainly avoid this person on some occasions because I prefer to *relax* with other friends.

A loving friendship or even a romantic relationship can change how you interact with the world. Psychologist Richard Davidson conducted a study (*1) which used brain imaging to track sixteen married women's responses to fear. Each individual woman was under the threat of electric shock. Let's say "Susan" is alone—that's when she experienced the most fear. Holding the hand of a stranger was a bit better for her. But holding her husband's hand significantly reduced Susan's feelings of fear and upset. How much of a reduction? Richard Davidson found that among the married women, the better the marriage, the more comforted the woman felt.

My point here is that it is vital for each person's strength and resiliency to have loving relationships. One of the best ways to make yourself resistant to pressure from an Opportunist or Guilter is to have loving relationships.

f) Be careful about what you hold as your identity.

Researchers note that some people hold impossible standards for themselves: they aim to "be perfect." Then they make an error. Perhaps they have overscheduled their lives and then find they must cancel some activity. They get down on themselves for disappointing someone. Then they get down on themselves for getting down on themselves! There is a solution: be careful about what you focus on as your identity.

What you hold as your identity will either build you up or tear you down. Do you identify yourself as a good friend? Do you allow your friends' approval to be a determining factor in your life? Sometimes your own friends will tear you down. For example, I was sometimes surprised by how friends and family teased me about my moniker as "America's Communication Coach" that describes what I do. If I mispronounced a word (perhaps when tired), I would be teased. But what kept me poised and strong was my understanding that my effectiveness and worth as a coach of speaking methods did not rest on my "being perfect."

In fact, every semester, with my graduate students in my

public speaking class, I begin with "We do not need you to be perfect; we do need you to be genuine."

Point to Remember:

Be careful about what you hold as your identity. Nurture your own self-esteem.

Your Countermeasure:

Start by keeping promises to yourself.

VULNERABILITY #2:
DO YOU FEEL GUILTY A LOT?
(10 Vulnerabilities to Spiritual Seduction)

At the end of one of my romantic relationships, my then-girlfriend guided us through our photos of shared memories [this was her therapist's idea]. Her heart was breaking and so was mine. Our tears flowed.

The tough part about relationships is that we never know if/when the end is coming. I wish I had "done better" during the relationship. I was faithful, but as an artist (author, speaker, film maker), I'm sure that I was distracted on a number of occasions. So I felt guilty after the relationship ended.

We can feel guilty for a good reason or just suffer some vague guilt feelings. Some religions emphasize our faults as human beings. The Guilters truly believe that guilt has an important use to force people to "behave in the right way."

We do NOT need to stay with the Guilter's opinion of "guilt." Now I'm suggesting another way to look at the situation:

- **Guilt:** a way of seeing one's behavior as horrible and interpreting a situation as static. The guilt is perpetual, as if the person is stuck with a permanent characteristic. How does that sound? Sarah describes herself with: "I'm always late. I'm lousy about time."

As opposed to . . .

- **"Sad, Amend, Make It Better" (SAM).** Another way I view this situation is: "Sad but resolved to do better." You can use this phrase to foster an empowered state of being. You take your sad feelings and use them as fuel to take action and to do better in the next similar situation. How? It's a process symbolized by these statements: "I made a mistake. I feel sad. I can make amends. I can make this better." This focus on "I can" is empowering and uplifting.

Numerous researchers and authors comment about how guilt causes damage. If you ask a friend about her experience of guilt, she is likely to reply: "I feel depressed about that mistake. And I feel drained of energy and ashamed." This is destructive. Why? It's holding a person back from making things better!

Guilt is anger directed at ourselves. — Peter McWilliams

This is a big problem. Have you noticed that people who are angry at themselves are *simply angry?* Some of them think they're accomplishing something by being angry at themselves. Not really. They're just remaining stuck. And their bad mood rubs off on others.

So drop guilt. Feel sad and then get busy making things better. It's good to face the truth as you notice something did not work. This is important feedback. You want something new and different. You do want something better. That means you're going to need to do something new and different.

The truth is for helping us amend our errors and pick up new disciplines. —Jim Rohn

If you made an error, you probably got results that hurt. Now focus on making amends and making up for the error. For many of us, it takes a new discipline to push past initial guilt feelings, find the sadness and use it as fuel. If you make an error and it causes unnecessary pain, then you can acknowledge that pain. Now you can commit to doing better next time.

For example, Sarah was repeatedly late in picking up her daughter after school. So she started a new discipline. Sarah started using two timers: one set for 30 minutes and the other set for 15 minutes before the time she needed to leave the office in order to be on time for her daughter. Now Sarah is free of feeling guilty for causing pain for her daughter. She notices that they lose less time in arguments. Sarah is on time so there is one less area of contention. They simply enjoy more of the time they share.

Let other pens dwell on guilt and misery. —Jane Austen

When we focus on "Sad, Amend, Make It Better (SAM)," we are in a mindset of hope and moving forward. Let other people glorify guilt as necessary for *them*. On the other hand, you can choose to respond to your own upset feelings, make a plan of action and stop digging yourself deeper in feeling disempowered. Climb out of a metaphorical hole of guilt.

No work or love will flourish out of guilt, fear, or hollowness of heart, just as no valid plans for the future can be made by those who have no capacity for living now. — Alan Watts

Guilt is about living in past regret and tearing oneself down in this moment. Enough! Choose "Sad, Amend, Make It Better" instead.

I think while all mothers deal with feelings of guilt, working mothers are plagued by guilt on steroids! — Arianna Huffington

If a working mother feels sad about missing time with her child, then let her use the "Sad, Amend, Make It Better" pattern. How can she see ways to make amends or make it better. Many mothers report that they feel exhausted and that they end up yelling at their kids. What can be a solution? Some mothers *devote energy* to making a circle of working mothers who "cover for each other" — that is, they can take turns in babysitting for each other. And they can recharge in simple ways: quiet time, reading, yoga class, an extended hot bath. Once they feel renewed, the mothers can give positive energy to their children when together.

To make amends and make things better, it takes resolve.

Resolve means I'll never give up. — Jim Rohn

Do you see how this is better than guilt?

Now let's cover Countermeasures to an Opportunist or Guilter who presses you to feel guilty.

a) Identify whether something was a "necessary ending."

Some situations, as well as some relationships, must come to a necessary ending. Some people discover that they had fallen in love with an image and not the actual person (for example). And it seems that some couples know that their romantic relationship must end but the only way they muster the energy to end it is to invent some self-righteous noise about how the other person is "wrong" or "bad." Not all relationships are meant to be a metaphorical "novel." Some are "short stories." And some relationships change form. Many of us attempt to cling to the status quo. It is a true life-skill to be able to flow and adapt to change.

b) Identify if you would give your friend the benefit of the doubt if he or she made a similar mistake.

My colleagues who are therapists tell me that it is amazing about how hard individuals are on themselves. Do you notice how you give more leeway to a friend? Have you said something like: "Don't be so hard on yourself. You were younger then. You had to learn the hard way." Extend the same kindness to yourself.

c) Allow that some things are "bumpy" or "messy" and "without closure."

At times, we may feel guilty about how a friend's feelings got hurt. The truth is, people's feelings get hurt and there are times that we are not the cause. Then what is the true cause? The person's interpretation of what had occurred. If Mandy invites Serina to her party, and Serina says, "I'm sorry. I'm pre-booked on that day," is it Serina's fault that Mandy feels rebuffed? No. In such a situation, the truth can be that this is a time when you cannot "make it all better."

How can you feel better even if you can't soothe your friend? Learn to get to the place of acceptance. During a recent session of my Comparative Religion class, I said, "Acceptance does NOT mean that you like it. It means that you don't fight it." This refers to the old phrase: "What you resist, persists."

When you stop resisting, a situation can "complete itself." How? Here's an example. Josh discovered how a disagreeable situation completed itself. One time, instead of defending himself when his wife criticized him, Josh replied, "You're right. Sometimes I do get distracted and don't devote full attention to listening to you. Please forgive me. I'll aim to do better. How about we talk after I take a shower?" His wife was surprised to hear Josh own up (and *not* resist) that he has made some errors. This was a start of a new chapter of their life together. Here we see how Josh made the situation better, and guilt feelings were *not* necessary.

Some people stubbornly insist that guilt is necessary. I have heard people say things like: "I need to feel guilty. It keeps me in line. It reminds me to do better next time."

Stop! How about we need to feel the sadness over the trouble that the error created. Then we use that sadness as fuel to make a plan and take action to make things better next time. How is sadness functioning as fuel? Let's face it. Many times, we need to feel discomfort to be motivated to improve a situation. But we do not need to feel guilty, like we're stuck with some trait (like "always late").

We return to the empowering pattern of "Sad, Amend, Make It Better."

Point to Remember:

Remember the power of "Sad, Amend, Make It Better (SAM)." Step away from disempowering guilt feelings.

Your Countermeasure:

Give yourself the benefit of the doubt and treat yourself like you would treat a good friend.

VULNERABILITY #3:
ARE YOU OVERLY IMPRESSED BY TITLES?
(10 Vulnerabilities to Spiritual Seduction)

In a number of organizations, people have a title like reverend, pastor, priest, father or doctor (of theology, for example). Just because someone has a title does NOT mean that they have resigned from the human race. They still have fallibilities. The news has often been filled with coverage of certain religious officials who have abused children. This behavior must not be tolerated and must be stopped. This is not theoretical to me: one of my friends was seduced, during his teen years, by a priest. One of my previous girlfriends was sexually assaulted. During that seven-year relationship, there were three people in the relationship: me, her, and her terrible memories of the predator of her childhood. The psychological damage continued for years. I have seen such damage to a relationship that childhood sexual assault causes. No organization should allow such evil acts perpetrated against children. Moving priests who committed crimes against children to other parishes is evil. Covering up such misconduct is evil. To fail to "clean one's own house" is evil.

All that is necessary for the triumph of evil is that good men do nothing. —Edmund Burke

Now we'll talk about countermeasures so that you can protect yourself from intimidation (or distraction) by someone's title.

a) Focus on the human being behind every title.
A human being can have blind spots, an overbearing ego and a lack of perspective. A misguided person with a title can also lack vital knowledge. Remember, it is still your responsibility to pause and deeply consider whether the person with a title has some lack of perspective or, Perhaps a hidden agenda. Devote yourself to seeking various appropriate sources of information. Do not only rely on a so-called expert.

b) Look upon every person as having value, including yourself.
Sure, a title like doctor may represent more book learning and perhaps the completion of specialized training. However, every human being is gifted with a special strength: the intuition. Book learning may indicate one solution to a problem, while intuition may suggest another. There are times when one needs to listen to one's own intuition. This became clear when a friend of mine had knee pain. A surgeon said, "Let's do exploratory surgery." My friend's intuition rang out: "Look for another way." My friend sought an opinion from a different specialist; it turned out that the pain had a different cause and it was merely

radiating to the knee. So exploratory surgery within the knee would have been a waste and it could have caused needless damage! So pay attention to your own intuition. If your intuition calls for a second or third medical opinion, gain those opinions. (Gaining multiple medical opinions is helpful, anyway.)

c) Take responsibility for yourself.
Researchers note that some individuals find it so difficult to stay in a state of uncertainty that they fail to devote effort and time to gather adequate information and reflect on options before making a decision. These individuals seek some form of relief from pressure and suffering. Just to get out of the anxiety to make a decision, a person may make a hasty, inappropriate decision. One way to release oneself from making a decision is to give up personal responsibility and hand it over to an "authority" or "expert."

But this is NOT for you. You can take responsibility and learn what you need to learn.

Here is another cautionary tale. "Corinne" has been plagued by health problems throughout her lifetime. But she has not made herself, through personal study, one of the most knowledgeable people on physical resiliency. She apparently avoids studying scientific advances and thought paradigms including psychoneuroimmunology. Her health status remains tentative with no energy and significant pain. Surely, it would be good to be proactive and do some research.

This example just reminds me to take action and focus on learning each day. In this way, life can be a constant adventure of learning and growing.

Point to Remember:

Regardless of a title, an expert is a human being who can have blind spots, an overbearing ego and a lack of perspective. This person may lack vital knowledge. So you must continue to take responsibility for your own life.

Your Countermeasure:

Take responsibility for yourself and get more learned opinions. Study, look into recent scientific advances, and devote time to reflecting on what you learn and your options. Use your intuition and mental faculties to assess any problematic situation.

VULNERABILITY #4:
DO YOU ACTIVELY LONG FOR FRIENDS?
(10 Vulnerabilities to Spiritual Seduction)

I admit that I was pulled (years ago) into two different religious organizations (mainstream) because I met cheerful, loving people who attended services. This is not necessarily a bad thing. To be attracted and pulled into an organization because of apparently friendly people is only natural.

However, a person who feels excessively lonely may, out of desperation for friends, change himself or herself to conform with "new friends at an organization." How might this person change himself? He might stifle his personal thoughts and preferences. He might let himself be dragged to all kinds of study groups when his heart longs for him to take classes and explore his own creativity. (We only have a small amount of discretionary time.)

Wanting friendship can be a healthy thing. I treasure my friendships and I have learned to support them effectively. Perhaps my interest in being a supportive friend has been partially fueled by watching my father drop his friends over the years. He is down to one friend.

On the other hand, feeling too lonely can make a person vulnerable to submerging the self to be a "nice package" to people at some religious organization.

At the center of your being you have the answer; you know who you are and you know what you want. —Lao Tzu

Don't let a desire for friendship tempt you to step away from "your center" and your true desires and goals of life. You need to avoid letting other people dictate what is good for your life. Why? Because only your intuition can illuminate your personal path.

Now we'll cover countermeasures to being vulnerable when actively longing for friends.

a) Find friends doing activities that you enjoy.

People are attracted to active people, those individuals going about their lives with positive energy. Do activities that you enjoy and then making friends will be a bonus. That is, you're not stuck doing activities you find have not intrinsic value to you. This strategy takes the desperation out of the equation. For example, on the occasion that friends have gathered for a drink at a bar, I've noticed a number of lonely people trying to put on a "happy face" when they exuded the body language of a lonely person. That's a lot of stress.

Instead, I have met people while joining friends for activities like hiking, visiting the Monterey Bay Aquarium and more. I've also enjoyed meeting new people at workshops and personal growth lectures.

When you are content to be simply yourself and don't compare or compete, everybody will respect you. —Lao Tzu

b) Learn what it takes to support friendships.

If you would take, you must first give, this is the beginning of intelligence. —Lao Tzu

Giving is also the beginning of friendships. If you want friends, the first thing to give is your attention. Be sure to listen to the other person. Help the other person see his or her valuable qualities. How? By expressing your appreciation. For example, just today, I congratulated a friend: "You took action. You decided that your book was complete. And you got it on Amazon.com. That takes courage."

As you can see, I expressed appreciation for her courageous action of putting her work out in the world. I could hear it in her voice: she really enjoyed my supportive comment.

To begin and continue friendships, you need to devote attention, patience and appreciation.

What is a key component of friendship? Your ability to effectively listen. In my book, *Be Heard and Be Trusted*, I talk about Three Listening Blockers:

1) *Judging*. Put your judgment on hold. Tell yourself, "I'll just listen. I don't need to agree or disagree" if you feel yourself getting uncomfortable while the other person is talking.

2) *Defending*. When you're defending yourself or some position, you have no space to listen to the other person. Start with listening. You could ask the person, "Is there anything else?" And keep on listening.

3) *"Me, too, One Up."* Many of us have been trained to show support by commiserating about a situation. We may say something like: "Yes, I agree it's tough taking four classes. I'm taking five classes." That is agreeing and then turning the spotlight of the conversation on yourself and going "one up" on the other person. Instead, say something that allows the person to feel her own feeling. It can sound like: "That sounds frustrating ('tiring' or 'like a strain'). So what happened next?" In this way, you keep your focus on the other person's story. You let the other person be "the star." That's when the other person feels like she has been heard and understood.

c) Go where the people are.
Author Robert H. Schuller told the story of how he learned to gain donations to build his Crystal Cathedral. A friend said, "When someone wants to bag a moose, he goes to where the moose are." So what did Robert H. Schuller do? He went to where wealthy people were—charity events and other functions.

So Now I'm inviting you to go where the people are. You could attend workshops, book signings, a lecture at a local Chamber of Commerce or some other event. Go to where like-minded people are. If you like science fiction books, you could attend a science fiction book discussion group meeting at a bookstore or go to a science fiction or comic book convention.

d) Take "baby steps."

I share a baby step with my graduate students who want to learn about networking skills. I often say, "Go to the buffet table. That's where the shy people are."

Talking with shy people is a baby step. After the students finish chuckling, I continue: "Then, when you say something like 'Look at all the desserts. What looks good to you?' The shy person thinks 'Whew! Someone has started a conversation with me.'"

Basically, when one talks with shy people, you become the "big fish in a small pond." Why? Because you're not competing with other people who are trying to talk with the celebrities and CEOs who are magnets of attention.

The idea is to expand your circle of acquaintances. So start "small" and talk with people who might welcome someone starting a conversation.

Point to Remember:

To begin and continue friendships, you need to devote attention, patience and appreciation; and be careful to nurture friendships so that you're not too lonely and vulnerable to spiritual seduction.

Your Countermeasure:

Do activities that you enjoy and find supportive friends along the way.

VULNERABILITY #5:
DO YOU CONSIDER YOUR APPEARANCE "BELOW AVERAGE"?
(10 Vulnerabilities to Spiritual Seduction)

Susan Boyle appeared as a contestant on the reality TV program *Britain's Got Talent* on April 11, 2009, singing "I Dreamed a Dream" from the musical *Les Misérables*. The video of her audition, as of this writing has been viewed 74,830,435 times.

A filmmaking colleague curtly said to me, "She looked frumpy. Her hairstyle was messy and her eyebrows were as thick as a man's."

Susan Boyle later underwent a "makeover." New hairstyle. Modified eyebrows. Flattering clothing. Her debut album, released in November 2009, rose to number one on music charts around the world.

Success is something you attract by becoming an attractive person. —Jim Rohn

We realize that people can be attractive in many ways: how they're supportive of other people, their kind smile and more. For example, even before her makeover, Susan Boyle had three attractive features: her belief in herself, her talent, and her sassiness.

My friend Joe had pleasant features. He was *not* a Hollywood leading man type. However, some time before his suicide, he did go on an extreme diet. Apparently, he thought he was not attractive enough as a chubby man. When he killed himself, he had a trim corpse. My point is that dieting and becoming thin were *not* enough for him to feel good about his life and himself. Appearance alone is not enough. Many of my treasured friendships began with no thought about appearance.

However, we can feel better about ourselves by taking some steps.

a) Realize that a smile brightens any face.

There's an old saying that what's on the inside affects what's on the outside. As a feature film producer and director, I have had opportunities to work with some extremely attractive (physically) models and actors. And guess what? When they're upset or angry or negative, it bleeds all over their face. They do not look attractive then. So continued attractiveness is not merely based on physical characteristics.

In addition, some of the most charismatic and attractive people I have met do not look like a model. They look pleasant, sure. But what really counts is that they make the person with them feel like the most important person in the room. People feel good just being near them. How do you get people to feel comfortable with you? Learn to smile as appropriate. That is, don't paste a "plastic smile" on your face. Smile naturally. Then let it naturally fade. And smile again—when the opportunity presents itself. Realize that your smile can be a welcoming start to friendships. You set people at ease.

b) If appropriate, get work done on your teeth.

In high school, I had an attractive girlfriend and . . . one of her front teeth had gone gray. I really didn't think about it much. But I remember some years ago seeing an old photo and there it was: the gray tooth. Other people have crooked teeth. If you have a concern here, you might find it valuable to save up the funds and devote some time, money and effort to improving your smile.

c) Find a flattering hair style.

It's embarrassing: the photo of my freshman year high school ID card has me looking like some nerd in a B-movie. It's like I'm trying too hard to fulfill the stereotype. Hair falling over my forehead and some dorky glasses. There was progress. By my senior year: it's contact lenses and a sharp haircut. My point is that a well-groomed hairstyle is helpful.

d) Energize your "aliveness."

Have you noticed that some people are just fun to be around? What is a common trait? Their "aliveness." They exude a positive energy. A number of people feel comfortable in the lively person's presence.

Everyone has an invisible sign hanging from their neck saying, 'Make me feel important.' Never forget this message when working with people. —Mary Kay Ash

Part of your aliveness is how you extend efforts to be kind to others.

If you want others to be happy, practice compassion. If you want to be happy, practice compassion. —Dalai Lama

Whether one believes in a religion or not, and whether one believes in rebirth or not, there isn't anyone who doesn't appreciate kindness and compassion. —Dalai Lama

My point is that we're not just attracted to the "live wire" people, the ones who command attention. We're also attractive to the people who pay attention and demonstrate they care for us.

We must have a theme, a goal, a purpose in our lives. If you don't know where you're aiming, you don't have a goal. My goal is to live my life in such a way that when I die, someone can say, she cared. —Mary Kay Ash

Yes, have a goal and a direction that you have chosen for your own life. Express passion and joy. A balance between compassion and passion reveals a person who has the zest for living.

Today I choose life. Every morning when I wake up I can choose joy, happiness, negativity, pain . . . today I choose to feel life, not to deny my humanity but embrace it. —Kevyn Aucoin

I have some friends who think that suffering is noble. They point to certain passages in the Bible to support their idea. As a comparative religion scholar, I also recall this passage: "This is the day the Lord has made; let us rejoice and be glad in it." (Psalm 118:24)

My point is *embrace all of life*. The joy and pain and the love you express.

An old phrase holds: "If you want love, show love."

Point to Remember:

Realize that smiling and nurturing your "aliveness" make you attractive.

Your Countermeasure:

Find ways to accentuate what you have and to express your "aliveness." Get a "makeover" of hair, teeth and wardrobe if you choose to. Make time to do enjoyable activities so you feel good about your life and yourself.

Tom Marcoux

VULNERABILITY #6:
DO YOU STILL SUFFER FROM
THE END OF A RELATIONSHIP?
(10 Vulnerabilities to Spiritual Seduction)

My friend Joe told me that he still regretted that he broke up with a former romantic partner some years ago. He said that he had wanted to play the field. I could see it in his face. He missed his former lover. I asked, "How about looking up the person on Facebook? Or LinkedIn?" Joe said, "No." I continued, "You might find the person free at this point. You might have good timing."

Throughout all the years I knew him, Joe refused to even give it a try. He was still suffering from the end of the relationship, but he was taking no action to reconnect with the former lover, nor was he doing any activities wherein he could meet new friends.

Here are countermeasures so that you can facilitate your recovery from the pain of a relationship breakup.

a) Identify what helps you feel proud of yourself.

When a relationship ends, it can be devastating. You gave yourself. You gave your best. It can feel like the person just threw you away in the trash.

When gloomy thoughts arise, it can help to say to yourself, "We didn't have a match." You realize that this particular person did not appreciate your value as a person. That is painful. But things are okay when you realize that your future can include someone else who will cherish being your friend or romantic partner. It's important to retain a faith in yourself and in all that is good inside you.

A faith is a necessity to a man. Woe to him who believes in nothing. —Victor Hugo

Believe in yourself and in the positive situations that are waiting for you in your near future. It may feel easier said than done. I'm with you about that. I have learned to use "easier said than done" as a stepping stone. So if it's tough, I take action to become tougher. Sure it can be heart wrenching to see a former lover walking on some street. I recall one big painful breakup in which my former lover requested that I forego walking in a particular neighborhood in San Francisco for one year. To be kind, I agreed. I have never seen her again and it has been more than 18 years. I'm certainly hoping that she has a whole new life and new love.

Meanwhile, to endure the ending of a relationship, do things to connect with your own value. Pull out your journal or write on sheet of paper and note *10 Things You're Proud of Yourself For*. You could keep a copy of the list in your wallet or purse.

Why is it helpful to view and review your list of *10 Things You're Proud of Yourself For*?

You need to counteract your amygdala (the part of your brain that searches for trouble), which tends to focus on any negative detail in your life. Instead, you must devote conscious effort to recall all that is working in your life.

This list can help you experience gratitude for what you do have in life.

b) Make space for grieving and healing.

When the love of my college days left my life, I was devastated. I knew that a "good cry" would help me but I was metaphorically collapsed in upon myself. Perhaps it's the socialization of a number of men in America that holds many of them from shedding tears.

Then two works of art came to my rescue. One was an episode of TV show *Mash* in which the character Hawkeye lost his love. I cried—a lot. Then later, when I saw feature film *Superman II*, starring Christopher Reeve, and Superman hypnotized Lois into forgetting their love affair leaving Superman to go his solitary way, I cried a great deal, too.

It was through crying and grieving that I could move forward with my life. It was my path to healing.

A number of authors, including Shakti Gawain, write about stepping into one's emotions and experiencing them. Some even speak about a "cleansing cry."

Try to approach God with your crying heart. It will awaken your soulful, spiritual consciousness. —Sri Chinmoy

At my friend Joe's wake, I felt tears on my face. I tossed a rose to join other roses in the ocean just outside San Francisco's Golden Gate Bridge. This was part of a ritual of letting go. It broke my heart to see the roses float away—just like Joe had left our lives. We would never see the roses nor

Joe again.

Make sure to make space for grieving. Partake in whatever healthy ritual that can help you cry. Perhaps see a sad movie (it worked for me). Maybe write a tearful letter and then burn it in a flame- and heat-proof container. Say goodbye as you rinse the ashes down the drain. Do what is necessary so that you can cry. This sadness is a path toward healing.

c) Treat yourself kindly, like you would support a grieving friend.

One thing you would probably do to support a grieving friend is listen. Get someone to listen to you. You could talk with a counselor. At the time of this writing, some local universities provide therapy by graduate students under the supervision of a licensed therapist. Some universities offer a sliding scale down to $10.00 for a session. Find some support for your grieving. And give yourself time. I recall seeing a trailer for the film *Rabbit Hole* in which an older character said, "At some point, it [grief] becomes bearable. It turns into something that you can crawl out from under and . . . carry around like a brick in your pocket." So give yourself some time.

Point to Remember:
Make space for grieving and healing.

Your Countermeasure:
Be sure to actually go through your grieving and treat yourself kindly.

VULNERABILITY #7: DOES YOUR SEXUAL ORIENTATION UPSET YOU?
(10 Vulnerabilities to Spiritual Seduction)

My friend Joe started to die when he joined a religious organization that was anti-gay so he had to hide his sexual orientation. He also suffered continued intolerance from his father who had disowned him. And the military discharged him when he joined with other gay people in the military who spoke up during the administration of President Bill Clinton. At the wake for my friend Joe, his family talked of the many citations for achievement he had earned during his years in the armed forces. If he had not been thrown out, he would probably still be alive today, serving in the armed forces and protecting the United States. And still, despite all of his efforts for gay people to be heard, he was not comfortable with being gay. One of his family members recently confirmed this.

Although this section directly relates to gay and lesbian readers, it is also relevant to any reader who has found it

difficult to "be oneself" and to "be different from the mainstream."

Here are some steps for a person to work with tough feelings about one's sexual orientation.

a) Find tolerant people—even if you need to move to another part of the country.

I was born and raised in San Francisco, and I have had the opportunity to develop friendships with people of various ethnicities, cultures and sexual orientations.

Because I am not gay, I interviewed my gay friends to gain some insight into their journey to self-acceptance related to sexual orientation.

One female friend said, "In the beginning, I felt that I would kill myself if someone found out. I didn't start to feel comfortable about my sexual orientation until I went to college and hung out with other gay people. I developed a community. Before that, I had felt so alone."

In addition, a number of friends told me that they found gay-friendly churches in San Francisco (for example).

Another friend said, "My second time away from the United States, when I went to London, I felt freer to express my sexuality. Maybe because I was so far from home. That was the beginning of feeling comfortable with my sexual orientation. When I went to New York I joined a group, Gay Circles, where gay men could talk about a number of issues. I began to feel comfortable about who I am."

In talking with my gay friends, I found three common themes:

1) They found people who were comfortable with their sexual orientation.

2) They found people with whom they felt comfortable

talking (some benefited from joining a support group).

3) They found some new friends. (people who were "like-minded" or "similar to me").

Rejoicing in our joy, not suffering over our suffering, makes someone a friend. —Friedrich Nietzsche

If you go out to be a friend, you'll find them everywhere. —Zig Ziglar

Finding supportive friends is helpful. Then you will be able to, as an old phrase holds, "plant yourself where you will blossom."

Some authors like Seth Godin talk about "your tribe." Your tribe comprises people with whom you have a natural connection. The word "tribe" does not necessarily mean a group related to Native Americans. It means something like "like-minded people."

'Most people' don't matter so much. You can't grow by going after 'most people.' —Seth Godin

On a number of occasions, I have heard friends complain about how "most people" exhibit some defect like prejudice, paying unequal wages for women and so many other maladies. I hear their concern. And, I notice that my friends do not interact daily with "most people." Instead, they talk with their own "tribe."

My point is that fretting about "most people" can be unproductive. And certainly for one uncomfortable with his or her sexual orientation, fretting about "most people" can be painful and stifling.

If you feel oppressed in some manner by "most people," there is a solution. You could identify what small corner of the world you want to make a bit better. Then you could look into taking some form of action. I know people who have chosen to volunteer some time to help. Some have helped at a soup kitchen; others have written a blog article or a book. Those interested in helping animals have volunteered at the Humane Society. What would you like to do?

You must be the change you wish to see in the world.
—*Mahatma Gandhi*

b) Develop a multi-faceted life to experience yourself as a full human being.

Who are you? Are you only your sexual orientation? A number of my gay friends celebrate many facets of their humanness. What do you like about yourself?

My coaching clients have written their own lists of what they like about themselves (in their personal journals). Some details include:
- I'm reliable.
- I'm trustworthy.
- I'm a true friend.
- I know how to forgive.
- I know how to restrain my sarcastic wit.
- I'm a loving person.
- I'm willing to face the reality of my mistakes and make amends for my mistakes.
- I'm creative.
- I'm artistic.
- I adapt well to tough situations.

Now help yourself to feel better. Write your own lists addressing:

a) What do you like about yourself?

b) What do you like in life? (This can be personal like you enjoy painting . . . or something you observe, like the artistry of ballroom dancers.)

c) What is going well in your current life?

d) What is your direction in life?

Review these lists. Really connect with what lights the fire behind your eyes.

c) Consider getting counseling (be careful about this).

To find a supportive counselor, it takes effort and willingness to move on if your intuition says, "Not this one." Pause and pay attention. You may notice that you two just "rub each other the wrong way." In addition, beware of some misguided counselors who try to "fix" you. Avoid them. Why? Some counselors have prejudices and agendas that can hurt you. Move on.

On the other hand, I have a personal coach who provides me with opportunities to think through tough decisions. That's helpful. I'm not looking for "great wisdom" to be bestowed by the personal coach. I'm looking for someone who *truly supports me in finding my own answers.*

As I have mentioned elsewhere, one can get counseling from a graduate student under the supervision of a licensed therapist. Once again, you're looking for someone who can help you voice your feelings and *find your own answers.* Why? Another person can only guess what will work for you. But you are "on the ground" in your own life. Only your intuition can illuminate your personal path in life.

Often, a great therapist, counselor or coach will help you

find better ways of taking action to feel better about yourself. Author Jeff Salzman said, "Therapy is for people who want to improve faster."

d) Find ways to accept who you are.

Recently, I was discussing Buddhism with my Comparative Religion class. Buddhists discuss the concept of "non-attachment." To approach life in a non-attached way is to be "non-demanding" that things go the way you prefer. Why? Because much of our lives we don't have direct control. For example, one person may be uncomfortable about his height or body type. Another person may be upset that certain people treat gays and lesbians as "less than." Here's what you can control: whether *you* practice self-acceptance. When you treat yourself in nurturing ways, you're less needy. And people respond better to less needy people.

Imagine how you would treat a cherished friend. Be that friend to yourself. Find ways to appreciate that you are alive, that you are drawn to whomever you're drawn to, and that you want to express love. Love is the starting point of true happiness. Elsewhere in this book I write about "to love is to be happy with." Another way to say this is find ways to be happy with your unique gifts and your positive efforts. Begin to love yourself.

Point to Remember:

Plant yourself where you will blossom. Find like-minded people and create your own circle of support.

Your Countermeasure:

Find your tribe. And in the meantime, find ways to accept yourself as you are.

VULNERABILITY #8: DO YOU FEEL A LACK OF HOPE OR ALIVENESS?
(10 Vulnerabilities to Spiritual Seduction)

Where does the feeling of hope come from? Let's begin with this quote:

Love in its essence is spiritual fire. —Lucius Annaeus Seneca

What about "a spiritual fire"? It is an expression of energy. And love empowers one's spirit. Do you love yourself? That's an essential question and on a profound level it relates to *how you identify your value as a person*. One time I comforted a friend who was crying because she didn't feel that she made a "contribution" to humankind. First, I heard her out. After much listening, I said, "If you weren't around Janet's life, my life, Steve's life, and your parents' life would be less. You bring so much to your loved ones." In essence, I was demonstrating that her life provided much value to her loved ones.

My point is love is a starting point for much of the hope we feel.

Our value as human beings can be much more than what we earn or do not earn in the marketplace. Do NOT let the culture dictate your value. So we can look at hope or aliveness as based on how you connect with other people and with your own creative expression as a human being. Humans create all of the time. They express love by listening to each other. They also creatively juggle the demands of life.

You were born with wings, why prefer to crawl through life?
—*Rumi*

I find listening to certain music gives me the feeling of soaring. Some people find that their iPod and purchasing songs from iTunes.com are excellent investments in enjoying life. Another way I feel great is to be immersed in conversation with good friends.

Earlier, I mentioned the phrase: *"Happiness is something to do, someone to love and something to hope for."* Now we have a starting point. By the way, I have noticed that people who are doing and loving, naturally find things to hope for.

Here are countermeasures.

a) Find something to do.

Participate! I know a couple of people who are retired. They're watching television from 9 AM in the morning until 11:30 PM. When I visit, I look at their faces. Are they happier now merely filling time with TV-viewing than when they had a job to go to? No!

You might ask: "How do you know that, Tom?" I'm observing their body language and facial expressions.

Instead, you can do better than wasting away in front of

the television: Find something to engage your mind and passion. Participate in life.

There are so many possibilities.
- Cooking classes
- Yoga
- Writing class
- Ballroom dancing
- Martial arts
- Tai chi (a slower form of martial arts)
- Volunteering to care for cats at the Humane Society
- and more

b) Find someone (or a pet) to love.

When you express your love to friends and family, you have new opportunities to feel connected.

One of the central ideas I share with my graduate students in my public speaking class is: "Make a transition from 'how am I doing?' to 'how are you doing?'" This means that someone stops being so self-conscious and become conscious of supporting the listener.

I have a number of people whom I call and ask: "How are things going for you?" This simple gesture of taking an interest in their lives has helped me build friendships.

I have also noticed that when I keep my own ego in check, I deepen friendships.

For example, I was at a gathering in which the group was talking about a film that we had just seen together. One person, "Malinda," was dominating the conversation. At some point, I saw the body language of "Janet," a shy and silent member of the group. She was sitting up and fiddling with her long hair. I knew that it was the perfect time to invite her to join the conversation. (Why? Because she had moved from her previous closed-in position on a chair in which she had her shoulders rounded and down.)

Later, Malinda confronted me with an intense tone as she said, "You shut me down. That hurt my feelings."

Now when I was confronted, like many of us, I felt my ego bruised. I was being accused of wrong-doing when I was simply trying to do something nice by looking out for a quiet member of the group.

Now here is how I deepened my friendship with Malinda. I did NOT defend myself by saying anything harsh. Instead, I took a deep breath and I quietly replied, "I didn't mean to shut you down. I just saw that I could bring Janet into the conversation. I'm concerned that your feelings were hurt. I was clumsy in how I tried to bring Janet in."

I continued to say mild things until I asked this question. "How do you feel that I could have said something better?" Eventually Malinda suggested, "You could have said, 'I'm looking forward to hearing your answer, Malinda, and when you're finished, I'd like to hear Janet's thoughts.'"

Since that time, I have practiced saying that phrase ("I'm looking forward to hearing your answer Malinda, and when you're finished, I'd like to hear Janet's thoughts.") multiple time to cement it in my memory. I even mentioned this process in my public speaking class. Why? I'm making sure the new option remains in my long-term memory.

My point is that keeping my ego in check and restraining myself from making negative replies is part of how I am loving and how I support my friendships. Yes—it takes work. And it's truly worth it. *Friendships are a great source of feeling hope and aliveness.*

About pets: In my 40's, I brought my first kitten into my life. To my sweetheart (she has had a number of cats), I said, "No cat in the bed." After the kitten had fallen asleep between my ankles, I said, "Isn't he cute!" Then, I lay there, trying not to awaken him. Even though I was the one who needed to rise early for work. (Go figure.)

c) Find something that brings lively moments to each day.

Yes—have lively moments *each day*. How? Put something fun into each day. Have something to look forward to. It doesn't need to take much time. And it can be something as simple as just five minutes, in your car, listening to soothing music. You rest and recharge your "batteries." I also use a digital video recorder connected to my TV to record funny shows like *Whose Line Is It, Anyway?* I make sure to watch something funny so I enjoy laughter on a daily basis.

If life is no fun, it is because you are no fun. Your life is always a reflection of what you are. Fun people lead fun lives. Don't argue with me—deal with it. Become more fun. Get friends who are more fun. Buy a joke book. Watch some funny movies.—Larry Winget

Have a list of positive people whom you can call on the phone. Schedule having a cup of coffee with a positive friend.

d) Realize the process for positive change.

To live full out and to enjoy your life, you will probably discover that you need to stretch and grow. To assist clients in their process towards change, I developed a special tool for when I coach people. It's called the M.O.S.T. process. I want the client to get the most from his or her interaction with me. Both the client and I need to measure the client's results and value gained. M.O.S.T. stands for:

M — Mindset moved
O — Open actions and complete them
S — Systems placed
T — Toolbox expanded

In my customized programs, I measure the progress of the client in all *four* areas noted above. For example, when I coach someone in excellent negotiation skills (revealed in my book *Darkest Secrets of Negotiation Masters*, free chapter visible at Amazon.com), I call this process "toolbox expanded" because the client learns new skills.

Furthermore, I help the clients put systems in place. By system, I mean a pre-set sequence of steps that helps the client accomplish an important process. For example, in sales, the client will preset what steps are needed to take a prospective client from the first call, through sending information, following up and closing the sale.

Now the client may not use the skills until one week after a series of coaching sessions has completed. Why? A situation like a specific negotiation may not arise during the period of coaching. But both my client and I know what value he or she has gained through the M.O.S.T. process.

I have given you an introduction to the M.O.S.T. process to show this bird's eye view of the process of permanent change.

I'll give you a simple example. I made a decision to drink more water and eliminate diet soda from my daily life.

1) *Mindset moved*
[I viewed data from a 2007 team of researchers from Harvard University, Brigham and Women's Hospital, Boston University School of Medicine, Tufts University and other top level institutions that noted that sugar substitutes

in diet soda apparently change one's hormonal balance—and a number of study subjects gained more weight on diet soda than the other groups in the study. The study concluded that the risk for developing a metabolic syndrome was 50 to 60 percent higher in the diet soda drinkers (*2). My mindset was moved.]

2) *Open actions and complete them.*
[When I talk about "open actions," I'm talking metaphorically about "opening a new door." My new actions were to replace drinking diet soda with water.

3) *Systems placed*
I realized that I had avoided drinking water because it was not fun. I needed a new system, so I started adding a splash of lemon juice to the water to provide a more enjoyable taste.

4) *Toolbox expanded*
I placed the bottle of lemon juice in an easily accessible part of the refrigerator door. My toolbox expanded in that *I consciously chose to make it easy to do the healthy thing for myself.*

My point in sharing the above example is to emphasize that when one has a systematic approach to changing one's behavior, the process becomes doable. To feel "alive!" you needs to feel healthy and capable. The above M.O.S.T. process can be adapted to any change you wish to accomplish. Remember, to feel hope and aliveness, you need to consciously take action to improve your own life. When you improve your own life, you're significantly less vulnerable to manipulation at the hands of an Opportunist or Guilter. You simply feel stronger.

Point to Remember:

Do not wait for anyone else to help you achieve "aliveness." Take action on your own behalf.

Your Countermeasure:

Make a plan. Enjoy some progress each day.

VULNERABILITY #9:
DO YOU EXPERIENCE ANY FORM OF MENTAL ILLNESS?
(10 Vulnerabilities to Spiritual Seduction)

My friend Joe had to deal with symptoms of clinical depression. He took his medication and attended sessions with a psychiatrist and therapist. Everyone was surprised when Joe committed suicide, including his family, friends, therapist and psychiatrist.

In the last month of his life, Joe visited me at my home two times, even though each roundtrip required six hours. The final time I saw him, I asked, "Do you want to get a cup of coffee or see a movie?" He replied, "No. I just want to sit here." He seemed content and comfortable.

Joe, obviously, felt the love in the home I share with my sweetheart. And he was probably silently saying goodbye to us.

One of the purposes of writing this book is to encourage you to pay attention to the symptoms of mental illness that may arise in you or people you know.

Dr. Gordon Livingston (*3) wrote:

"People with serious mental illness—schizophrenia, bipolar disorder, major depression—are generally so affected by their symptoms (for example, hallucinations, paranoia, manic behavior, debilitating sadness) that there is no mistaking their distress. They generally require medication, and people around them are aware that they have a profound organic illness. Those with so-called personality disorders, however, are frequently undiagnosed and may be unaware that anything in their behavior is abnormal. In fact, they frequently believe that their interpersonal difficulties are the fault of others or society as a whole. This idea undermines people's motivation to change even when it is obvious that their lives are not working in some important respect."

So please pay close attention to the next paragraphs because you might save a loved one's life or even your own life. Spiritual Seduction pushed my friend Joe toward suicide and he died with an open religious book next to him. The religious organization that he worked for condemned his homosexuality and he felt it necessary to hide his sexual orientation while he continued to work there. I can only imagine how much stress he felt on a daily basis.

a) Seek medical information and medical advice if appropriate.

According to the National Institute of Mental Health, symptoms of depression may include the following:
- Difficulty concentrating, remembering details, and making decisions
  - Fatigue and decreased energy
  - Feelings of guilt, worthlessness, and/or helplessness

- Feelings of hopelessness and/or pessimism
- Insomnia, early-morning wakefulness, or excessive sleeping
- Irritability, restlessness
- Loss of interest in activities or hobbies once pleasurable, including sex
- Overeating or appetite loss
- Persistent aches or pains, headaches, cramps, or digestive problems that do not ease even with treatment
- Persistent sad, anxious, or "empty" feelings
- Thoughts of suicide, suicide attempts

According to an article at WebMD.com,

"Depression carries a high risk of suicide. Anybody who expresses suicidal thoughts or intentions should be taken very, very seriously. Do not hesitate to call your local suicide hotline immediately. Call 1-800-SUICIDE (1-800-784-2433) or 1-800-273-TALK (1-800-273-8255)—or the deaf hotline at 1-800-799-4TTY (1-800-799-4889).

"Warning signs of suicide with depression include:

- A sudden switch from being very sad to being very calm or appearing to be happy
- Always talking or thinking about death
- Clinical depression (deep sadness, loss of interest, trouble sleeping and eating) that gets worse
- Having a "death wish," tempting fate by taking risks that could lead to death, like driving through red lights
- Losing interest in things one used to care about
- Making comments about being hopeless, helpless, or worthless

- Putting affairs in order, tying up loose ends, changing a will
- Saying things like "It would be better if I wasn't here" or "I want out"
- Talking about suicide (killing one's self)
- Visiting or calling people one cares about

"Remember, if you or someone you know is demonstrating any of the above warning signs of suicide with depression, either call your local suicide hot line, contact a mental health professional right away, or go to the emergency room for immediate treatment."

My friend Joe's suicide has deeply affected me. In fact, within two months of Joe's death, I asked a close friend, "Do you need a suicide watch?" Now asking that question felt like a big risk because a number of people get angry if someone implies that they're having trouble coping with tough parts of life. But I felt it important that I ask while I saw my friend dealing with a big traumatic part of his life. By the way, a suicide watch entails friends and family taking shifts and making sure that the person has someone with him or her throughout the day.

I know someone, "Alfonso," who was suicidal. The good news is that his friends gathered and conducted a suicide watch. They remained with Alfonso during his time of need. And he is still alive and well now 15 years later.

Recently, I was at a gathering of friends and I happened to overhear two friends talking. This is an example of how we can support friends through crises. One friend opened up and spoke of her clinical depression symptoms, and the other friend said, "You can call me. Just be specific. If you're having suicidal thoughts, let me know. I'll be there for you."

b) Find out if a combination of talk therapy and medication is helpful for you.

I have a couple of dear friends who are dealing with their own clinical depression. They tell me that a combination of talk therapy plus medication has been helpful for them. They say that the medication does not make them feel good; it merely gets them to a baseline. That is, instead of feeling depressed, they feel "neutral" but not good. The talk therapy is helpful for them to think through ways of coping with the depression symptoms. For example, many people dealing with depression symptoms find that exercise is a crucial part of their self-care processes. So I invite you to consider your alternatives including talk therapy plus medication plus exercise, if you're facing some form of mental illness.

A special note: My friends who deal with depression symptoms often say that they are "depressed people." I suggest the term "person dealing with depression symptoms." Why? In this way, one does *not* paralyze one's thinking as a static, always oppressed "depressed person." The truth is the symptoms vary day-to-day and even hour-to-hour. It's empowering to think of oneself as a "spiritual being first" who is dealing with depression symptoms.

c) Make multiple efforts.

One of my friends had a counselor in high school who did such a poor job that she was extremely resistant to seeing a therapist and psychiatrist. It was as if she had been conditioned to look upon counselors as the "enemy." Still, her friends made multiple efforts to support her in getting a therapist and psychiatrist with whom she could feel comfortable. Now after ten years of effort, my friend is still alive and doing much better today than she was ten years ago.

If you're also suffering from any of the symptoms described above, please get help as soon as possible. We need you to take care of yourself. As you saw above, some suicidal people put others at risk. If a person drives through a red light, other motorists may lose their lives, too.

I believe in getting help. I have had a personal coach for 14 years and I participate in a monthly meeting of a Mastermind Group (professionals who share support and practical ideas).

Getting help is honorable and advised. *We need each other. We fit like jigsaw puzzle pieces.* If appropriate, get the help you need.

Point to Remember:

Seek medical attention and therapy if appropriate. Realize that numerous individuals increase happiness and productivity through a combination of talk therapy and medication.

Your Countermeasure:

Take responsibility for getting assistance and take action, if you believe you need help with mental difficulties.

VULNERABILITY #10:
DO YOU FEEL YOU CAN'T GET A GOOD NIGHT'S SLEEP?
(10 Vulnerabilities to Spiritual Seduction)

If you feel that you're getting poor sleep or not enough sleep, please seek medical attention. Why? People who don't sleep well exist in a weakened state, which makes them vulnerable to manipulation. Don't let this happen to you.

I know personally that medical intervention for improving sleep can change a person's whole life. For example, my sweetheart uses a CPAP machine to deal with sleep apnea. CPAP stands for "Continuous Positive Airway Pressure." The machine is not too loud; I sleep next to her. She told me, "Upon first using the machine, I felt so much more rested. It makes a big difference! I can do more and I have so much more energy."

a) Get help related to sleep disorders.

At WebMD.com, the symptoms of [the sleep disorder] sleep apnea are described as:

"• Loud, persistent snoring
• Pauses in breathing, accompanied with gasping episodes when sleeping
• Excessive sleepiness during waking hours"

To find out if you actually have sleep apnea, you need to participate in a sleep study. You go into the medical facility and they place sensors on your face and other places to monitor your vital signs and more while you sleep. I know two people who have gone through the process and both mentioned how surprised they were about being able to fall asleep in such an environment.

Sleep disorders include (as mentioned by the National Institutes of Health):

"• Insomnia—a hard time falling or staying asleep
• Sleep apnea—breathing interruptions during sleep
• Restless legs syndrome—a tingling or prickly sensation in the legs
• Narcolepsy—daytime "sleep attacks"

[And] Nightmares, night terrors, sleepwalking, sleep talking, head banging, wetting the bed and grinding your teeth [which] are kinds of sleep problems called parasomnias."

It really helps people to put effort into making sure to get a good night's sleep. According to the National Institutes of Health (nih.gov): "There are treatments for most sleep disorders. Sometimes just having regular sleep habits can help."

My point is that people with sleep difficulties live day to day in a weakened state. The weakened person has difficulties in thinking, standing up for oneself, and maintaining focus. An Opportunist or Guilter can easily take advantage of the over-tired person. Strengthen yourself by ensuring that you sleep well.

b) Try a Daily Journal of Victories and Blessings.

Feeling unsettled just before you go to bed can affect the quality and quantity of your sleep. For example, in college I would go to bed unhappy. Why? I felt like I was losing a battle; my to-do list would not get smaller (Perhaps my double-major had something to do with that and also my working my way through college). After college, I began a practice that I have done for years. Every night, I write in my *Daily Journal of Victories and Blessings*. I define a Victory as something that I accomplished. It can be as simple as taking a 45-minute walk with my sweetheart. A Blessing is something pleasant like a surprise phone call from a friend.

It isn't until you come to a spiritual understanding of who you are—not necessarily a religious feeling, but deep down, the spirit within—that you can begin to take control. —Oprah Winfrey

When you write down your Victories and Blessings, you discover that you are actually blessed in your life.

Writing down the blessings of my life reconnects me with my faith that there is a Higher Power looking out for me. This is truly comforting when it's time to go to sleep.

c) In 2 minutes, write your Top Six Targets.

Some people stay tense at bedtime because they fret about possibly forgetting something important for the next day's work. Take two minutes and write down your *Top Six Targets*. These are your most important tasks. I often say,

"Two [tasks] for you, two for family and two for work." We can't do everything. But we can do the most important tasks. When you have your list of Top Six Targets, you have your marching orders for the next day. Upon awakening, take that list in hand and make the best of your new day.

Point to Remember:

Appropriate sleep and rest are the basis of good mental and physical health.

Your Countermeasure:

Study what is necessary for you to get good sleep. Take action if necessary.

CONCLUSION TO BOOK I

We have covered vital information about the *10 Vulnerabilities to Spiritual Seduction:*

1) Do you experience low self-esteem?
2) Do you feel guilty a lot?
3) Are you overly impressed by titles?
4) Do you actively long for friends?
5) Do you consider your appearance "below average"?
6) Do you still suffer from the end of a relationship?
7) Does your sexual orientation upset you?
8) Do you feel a lack of hope or aliveness?
9) Do you experience any form of mental illness?
10) Do you feel you can't get a good night's sleep?

My friend Joe suffered from seven of the above:

- He felt guilty a lot.
- He considered his appearance "below average."
- He still suffered from the end of a relationship.
- His sexual orientation upset him.

- He felt a lack of hope and aliveness.
- He experienced a form of mental illness.
- He couldn't get a good night's sleep.

If this book existed, Joe could have, perhaps, used the contents to strengthen himself. I miss my friend. I hope that this book brings blessings to many people. That would be something good to accompany my memories of my dear friend.

In addition to helping you protect yourself from manipulation by Opportunists and Guilters, my goal is to help you enjoy life more often.

Man cannot live without joy; therefore when he is deprived of true spiritual joys it is necessary that he become addicted to carnal pleasures. —St. Thomas Aquinas

Later in this book, we will discuss the Divine Gifts that will assist you in developing happiness.

Happiness cannot be traveled to, owned, earned, worn or consumed. Happiness is the spiritual experience of living every minute with love, grace, and gratitude. —Denis Waitley

The great awareness comes slowly, piece by piece. The path of spiritual growth is a path of lifelong learning. The experience of spiritual power is basically a joyful one. —M. Scott Peck

In the next section, we will discuss the Darkest Secrets of Spiritual Seduction Masters.

Let's move forward . . .

BOOK II:
DARKEST SECRETS OF SPIRITUAL SEDUCTION MASTERS
(THE DARK SEDUCER'S METHODS AND YOUR COUNTERMEASURES)

We began with the *10 Vulnerabilities to Spiritual Seduction*. Now we'll continue with actual methods that Opportunists and Guilters use to lead people around. Remember, Opportunists are those people who do not believe in a helpful spiritual path and only use religious talk to manipulate others and pluck money from their wallets and purses. Guilters are devout people who believe that people need to feel guilty and horrible—and to fear punishment from God (*their view* of God). Guilters often claim to be the go-between between people and Higher Power. The idea of "go-between" ranges from the TV evangelist who requests that the viewer place his or her hand on the TV screen to the priest who insists that the sacrament of Confession is a necessary part of people's lives—and other rules of some religions.

Now we will continue with the Darkest Secrets of Spiritual Seduction Masters, that is their actual methods.

- S—Submerge your self-esteem.
- E—Encourage self-loathing.
- D—Deny your intuition.
- U—Undermine your ability to hold two opposing thoughts.
- C—Comfort you with "friends."
- E—Eliminate your support system.

DARK SEDUCER'S METHOD #1: SUBMERGE YOUR SELF-ESTEEM
(6 Dark Seducer's Methods)

How does an Opportunist or Guilter submerge a person's self-esteem?

Have you ever heard someone say:

"You have committed a sin. You are unpleasing to God."

or

"You are all sinners. There is nothing you can do of yourself. Only the grace of God can save you from the vile sin you have committed."

or

"You have the stain of sin on you. Nothing imperfect enters heaven."

For people who believe the above, the blow to their feelings about themselves simply hurts. It is also scary to feel that one is liable to be eternally punished. And, let's face it, such beliefs can trash one's self-esteem.

As I mentioned earlier, one definition of self-esteem (from author Nathaniel Branden) specifies:

"Self-esteem is the disposition to experience oneself as being competent to cope with the basic challenges of life and of being worthy of happiness. It is confidence in the efficacy of our mind, in our ability to think. By extension, it is confidence in our ability to learn, make appropriate choices and decisions, and respond effectively to change. It is also the experience that success, achievement, fulfillment—happiness—are right and natural for us."

Now that's a good start for this present discussion. Let's face it together: if your self-esteem is low you're in great pain. And such pain can make a person desperate for relief. The Opportunist or Guilter runs in to fill the void. They continuously hammer home ideas like: "Of course, you feel bad, you are 'broken and in exile.'" Then they offer a salve that sounds like: "If you follow these [rules], then and only then you will be pleasing to God."

You yourself, as much as anybody in the entire universe, deserve your love and affection. —Buddha

Whatever you are doing, love yourself for doing it. Whatever you are feeling, love yourself for feeling it. —Thaddeus Golas

It is reported that Jesus, the Christ, said, "Love your neighbor as yourself." And it appears that we need to learn how to love and nurture ourselves.

Now we'll explore countermeasures to Opportunists' and Guilters' efforts to submerge your self-esteem.

a) Immerse yourself in uplifting music.

Our scientific power has outrun our spiritual power. We have guided missiles and misguided men. —Martin Luther King, Jr.

I realize upon hearing a quote like this some readers would think that this doesn't apply to them because they (not being world leaders) don't aim physical missiles. But there are other weapons people use on each other: words and the tonality with which we speak. You have the power to affect people right next to you. How? With your mood. Ever stand next to someone who was in a bad mood? It was like you were hit with waves of sludge. Ugh! And that's how your soul responds to a constant diet of "bad news." You're weighed down. It's like wearing eyeglasses covered in sludge and you can't see the good things in life.

The solution? Have a daily "broadcast media-free zone." Step away from TV, radio, email, Facebook, and Twitter—and *enjoy some soothing music.* Why? This gives you a break to refresh yourself.

Music washes away from the soul the dust of everyday life. —Berthold Auerbach

Along the lines of giving your mind and soul a break, consider taking five to twenty minutes of quiet time or meditation. As authors like Deepak Chopra say, "Go to the silence. Connect with the field of pure potentiality . . . Experience inner peace as you meditate."

News broadcasts (and certain websites) that provide a steady diet of war, crime and tragedy cloud our perception of the blessings in the world of love, compassion and kindness.

Instead of subjecting yourself to a constant barrage of doom-filled "news," take at least five minutes a day to immerse yourself in soothing music . . . or even enjoy some quiet time.

b) Realize that your worth is not only built on specific accomplishments.

Low self-esteem is like driving through life with your handbrake on. —Maxwell Maltz

That's a powerful idea. And I want to emphasize that a person needs a "basic faith" in himself or herself. Why? Because I have firsthand experience listening to some clients who think badly about themselves because *they* say that they "haven't accomplished much."

Really? I notice that they seem to only value career-oriented accomplishments. A human being is so much more than his or her job. How about being a kind and supportive friend?—that's important. That is a valuable accomplishment.

Then some of my clients reply, "Oh yeah? No one pays you for that. Society doesn't value . . ." Wait a minute. Society? Are we talking about that vaporous "they"? As in "they don't care about people being nice"?

Some people complain about how "society" limits them, but they may be focusing on only one small corner of the big picture. I have a client who constantly complains about the lack of opportunities for women. However, if she would look at her own life, she will see that she has done what she wants to do. She did not get married and have children like her mother preferred. She got an advanced degree. And she has traveled the world, often in dangerous places and by herself. She didn't let fear of bodily injury stop her. She has not let society dictate what she can do with her own life. But she glosses over that and emphasizes the thoughts of certain "other people" [by which she means her mother and anyone else who frowns on her "independent lifestyle"].

Well, we all know that self-esteem comes from what you think of you, not what other people think of you. —Gloria Gaynor

And so I invite you to find your own self-worth outside of any stereotypical, so-called society's point of view of what is valuable.

Consider starting from a position of basic faith in yourself: "I'm a good person. I'm learning every day. I'm finding ways to be good to people."

One should not think about the result; one does not travel to reach a destination, but to travel. —Johann Wolfgang von Goethe

I know some of my friends would argue that we have a destination in mind when considering traveling to work. But the point here is: *how* do you travel? Are you mindful of each present moment?

Think about it. Do you do things in your life because that actual *process of doing is valuable?* For example, I write books, not just for the result of many people purchasing the books, but also for my deepening as a human being. That is, as I write a book, I learn, I synthesize information and I explore. My thinking boundaries expand. I enjoy the process. *Which of your activities do you do in which you enjoy the process?*

I believe in one God, and no more . . . My own mind is my own church. —Thomas Paine

What are you doing with your own mind? Are you making it strong so it won't be vulnerable to an Opportunist or Guilter? It is up to *you* to guard what you tell yourself.

Realize that every time you say "I am" or "I have," you are programming yourself.

Your power is in your choices of programming yourself.

The idea of programming yourself relates to the self-fulfilling prophesy. Some of my college students say that they are not good at remembering names. And they give up and put no effort into it. So as a self-fulfilling prophesy, they actually fail to remember names.

On the other hand, I have met individuals who say they have a good memory. And through their day, *they find examples* when they have remembered something valuable. They talk about their successes. In essence, they are programming themselves. How? A person who says she has a good memory is likely *to pay closer attention* to details like someone's name.

Let's continue exploring self-programming. You can program your thoughts, which often lead to your actions by using affirmations (positive, present tense and personal statements). You can state affirmations out loud or repeat them in your mind throughout your day. If you say the following affirmations, you strengthen yourself:

- I am a good friend.
- I am learning every day.
- I am a good person.
- I have good intentions and I act in support of other people.
- I am creative.

Here is another affirmation: "Higher Power has given me inherent goodness and talents that I use well."

I have written (elsewhere in this book) that my happiness comes from "I know who I am. I know what I want. And I know what direction I'm going in." You can notice that I am not merely basing my self-esteem on accomplishments. That is, I'm **not** saying, "I'm happy because I have written 22 books and I directed a feature film that is in international distribution." Instead, I focus on enjoying my process of living, not merely what I have accomplished. Accomplishments are important, but living well is more important to me.

The most precious things in life are not those one gets for money. —Albert Einstein

Like what precious things? Love. Friendship. Learning.

Where there is no vision, the people perish. —Proverbs 29:18

I invite you to have your own vision of yourself. How are you approaching each day of your life? What are your principles or code of conduct? You are *not* merely your accomplishments. The idea of "you are your accomplishments" aligns with the notion of you as "a human 'doing.'" You are a human being . . . and a spiritual being. Let's return to this quote:

We are not human beings having a spiritual experience. We are spiritual beings having a human experience. —Pierre Teilhard de Chardin

Some authors, including Dr. Wayne Dyer, say that each

person has some divinity in him or her and therefore the person's essence is good and valuable. Dr. Wayne Dyer points out that a drop of ocean water retains the identity of the whole ocean—like we are part of the Divine.

In my recent comparative religion college class, I talked about non-attachment. And I was thinking about my friends who are approaching 50 years old and have told me that they do not feel good, due to "not having accomplished much." These are my same friends who do not attend their high school or college reunions out of apparent embarrassment. I find this sad. It seems that they are "too attached" to basing their worth on job-related accomplishments.

Practice "non-attachment" to the idea that one is a valuable person based only on job-related accomplishments. Let's use a different scale than merely job-related accomplishments. How about a scale related to the following ideas:

To laugh often and much; To win the respect of intelligent people and the affection of children; To earn the appreciation of honest critics and endure the betrayal of false friends; To appreciate beauty, to find the best in others; To leave the world a bit better, whether by a healthy child, a garden patch, or a redeemed social condition; To know even one life has breathed easier because you have lived. This is to have succeeded. —Ralph Waldo Emerson

I suggest that if you have been kind to others (and yourself) you have contributed to the joy on this planet. That is an important process of living a valuable life.

Here is a simple example of making a positive contribution to another person's day. At any networking event, the person who listens well to a new acquaintance is appreciated. Listening is a compassionate and supportive act. And it does not depend on having completed "grand accomplishments." However, listening is one of the great things we do for each other.

c) Clarify the difference between self-esteem and "vain pride."

I really want to support you in taking action to raise your self-esteem, despite what you may have heard in faulty definitions of self-esteem. Self-esteem is not vain pride. Look what self-esteem can do:

There is overwhelming evidence that the higher the level of self-esteem, the more likely one will be to treat others with respect, kindness, and generosity. —Nathaniel Branden

Let's look at the difference between self-esteem and vain pride. I have heard some parents say things like: "Don't keep on talking about what you've done. Don't get a fat head." These parents want their children to avoid vanity, what I would call "vain pride." And that sounds good.

Now let's take our discussion into how "vain pride" relates to spiritual seduction. If an Opportunist says, "Beware of pride. Do not talk of your 'good works.' It's only your relationship with God that counts. And remember, you must attend Sunday services . . ." then the Opportunist is taking advantage of the confusion between self-esteem and vain pride.

Let's boil down the difference between self-esteem and vain pride:

• Self-esteem is: "I am capable, and I can get better with more training."

- Vain pride sounds like: "I got this. I don't need anybody's help. (I'm special.)"

Vain pride and self-delusion often arise together. When someone talks of "too much self-esteem," it can be really about "vain pride and self-delusion." For example, some studies warn of "too much self-esteem." These studies discuss how some people overestimate their skill levels. However, I suggest that we're *not* talking about "self-esteem"; we're really talking about *self-delusion* if someone has an inaccurate picture of their skills and talent.

So the solution falling into self-delusion is to get useful, reliable feedback from people you trust. Then you can avoid self-delusion. As one of my editors said, "Writing is a two person process." An editor can catch things that the writer misses because the writer's brain fills in gaps. The editor easily sees the missing details that a reader would require.

Along the lines of avoiding self-delusion, let's return to a topic I mentioned earlier: humility. Humility is useful even when one achieves a goal. Why? Because to perform at the level of excellence, one needs to constantly improve and overcome any bad habits that impair such a high level of performance.

Success is a lousy teacher. It seduces smart people into thinking they can't lose. — Bill Gates

Sometimes, in my graduate level public speaking class, I say, "Be coachable. Prepare daily for a home run." In summary, nurture your self-esteem (your belief in your capacity) and guard yourself from self-delusion and from those Opportunists or Guilters who would like to tear you down. Why do they tear people down? To make them dependent. But this is NOT for you. Keep learning and keep growing.

d) Watch your own level of emotional pain and desperation—and engage in self-nurturing efforts.

Are you watching more TV? Are you overeating? Observe your own behavior and you'll have an idea about your level of emotional pain. How? People seek to numb themselves when they have a significant level of pain.

Over the years of working with clients and audiences, I have noticed that people need a balance between activity and rest. When we're in emotional pain we may fall back on "self-numbing" activities like television watching or eating to fill voids in our lives.

Earlier I spoke of how over-focusing on accomplishment can warp one's self-esteem. Now here is the other side of the coin. Making incremental progress can raise your self-esteem.

Nothing builds self-esteem and self-confidence like accomplishment.—Thomas Carlyle

The idea is to hold things in balance. Avoid overwork and too much numbing behavior. Instead, make small promises to yourself. Earlier, I mentioned having a plan of reading just two pages a day. With a small promise, you are more likely to fulfill your plan. Then you'll feel good.

My point is that we need to have a deep well of basic faith in ourselves (and for many of us, a faith that Higher Power is helping us) so that so-called failures do *not* devastate us. Some people try to "hide" to avoid disappointments. The truth is: *Disappointments come along whether we reach for our dreams or not.*

Many times I've been asked, 'What if I try really hard, but my dreams still don't come true?' This is always my answer: In the end, do you think you'll be happier if you've lived your life pursuing your dreams or suppressing them? Dream big. Life is short. Amp it up! —Kim Marcille Romaner

Along the way, most people endure some big disappointments. To keep moving forward, ask yourself some empowering questions and note your answer in a personal journal:

1) What have I learned here?
2) Did I enjoy the ride (the process of creating whatever you were working on)?
3) How can I do it better next time?
4) What gaps are in my knowledge? Who can help me do better?

These questions serve as a starting point. The next step is to stay alert about how it takes energy to keep going despite disappointments. The way to keep moving forward has two parts:

a) Monitor your level of emotional pain and desperation.
b) Increase your self-nurturing efforts.

How do you nurture yourself?
Here are possibilities:
- Listen to music
- Take a walk in nature
- Write in your journal
- Practice tai chi
- Yoga
- Watch a funny TV show
- Play the piano

- Read a book
- Paint a picture
- And more.

Find your own ways to nurture yourself. And be prepared to experiment. What brought joy earlier in life may not fit at this moment. One of my clients bounced from sculpture, to painting, to building Lego structures while listening to music.

Point to Remember:
Opportunists or Guilters use lowering your self-esteem to make you desperate for some emotional relief.

Your Countermeasure:
Take action to enhance your own self-esteem. Carefully choose what you base your positive feelings upon. Do you only focus on career-related achievements? What about other facets of your life? How are your relationships? Have you been taking good care for yourself? Do you provide yourself with times of rest and renewal? Devote some moments daily to something that you enjoy (perhaps a hobby).

DARK SEDUCER'S METHOD #2: ENCOURAGE SELF-LOATHING
(6 Dark Seducer's Methods)

How does an Opportunist or Guilter get a person to experience self-loathing?

Some Opportunists and Guilters proclaim:

"God hates the sinner. You are not fit to be in His sight."

or

"God's perfect justice will be met unto you who have allowed your base animal behavior to run rampant."

For a believer of the above, to make mistakes or to experience sexual urges is supposedly base and vile.

Belief in a cruel God makes a cruel man. — Thomas Paine

I'm repeating this powerful quote here because it applies to the self-cruelty I viewed in a believer, that is a former girlfriend. When fervently praying, she would have a terrible look of anguish on her face. She closed her eyes tightly, with her face creased in pain. During our conversations, I got the clear impression that she felt guilty for her past behavior. But she said that she felt cleansed and that she had started over. *That's what she said.* But her demeanor displayed that she still felt unworthy and still hated herself for her imperfections. Her thought patterns appeared to be a *cruel* affliction on her present day feelings. Apparently she believed in a cruel God, and she was cruel to herself. She was not finding solace in connecting with her interpretation of God. Her upset moods caused me discomfort, too. Anyway, she soon ended our relationship.

I mention being cruel to oneself because it is a major element of self-loathing. *The Merriam-Webster Dictionary* defines *loathe* as "to dislike greatly and often with disgust or intolerance." *Disgust* and *intolerance* slap a person down. That's not spiritual nourishing. Self-loathing is a powerful phenomenon. An Opportunist or Guilter wants you to feel self-loathing. Why? Then he or she can arrive on the metaphorical white horse and save you from feeling empty and upset. It's like someone giving you salty potato chips. Soon, you're thirsty; and predictably you'll be searching for something to drink. The Opportunist or Guilter will be happy to provide you with the "drink"—the beliefs they want you to swallow.

The path to self-loathing includes two self-sabotaging mistakes (noted by Minister and lecturer Duke Robinson): trying to be perfect and taking on too much. He suggests that we choose to "look at life through the lens of love. In other words, you decide to see acceptance—rather than punitive judgment and rejection—at the beginning, middle and end of your life."

Along these lines, we can see self-loathing as a rejection of the self. And it does not work to help in improving a person's life. Who do you think overcomes a negative habit of being late (for example)—the person who accepts herself or the person who rejects herself? The person who accepts herself has more energy to *compassionately look at her errors and do something about them.*

On the other hand, the person who rejects herself will probably avoid the whole topic of lateness in her thinking. She'll continue to mindlessly maintain her bad habits that lead to being late time and again. And, she is probably exhausted from beating herself up emotionally.

If you had a person in your life treating you the way you treat yourself, you would have gotten rid of them a long time ago.
—Cheri Huber

Self-esteem is as important to our well-being as legs are to a table. It is essential for physical and mental health and for happiness. —Louise Hart

When an Opportunist cuts down your self-esteem, it's like they're leaving you with no leg to stand on. The Opportunist influences you to feel disgust and intolerance toward yourself, and that is deeply damaging to your psyche. I have noticed that some of my friends who spend much time in guilt and fearful thoughts (related to their personal spiritual path) are among the physically sickest people I know. They tell me that there is value in "offering up suffering" to help others. And you know what? They have a lot of suffering to offer up! It appears to be a self-fulfilling prophesy.

As I was looking up the research about the long-term effects of self-loathing, I made this connection: Opportunists and Guilters are in effect *bullying* their followers.

Mark Dombeck, Ph.D, wrote:

"The experience of being bullied can end up causing lasting damage to victims. This is both self-evident, and also supported by an increasing body of research. . . . For the most part, physical damage sustained in a fist fight heals readily. . . . What is far more difficult to mend is the primary wound that bullying victims suffer, which is damage to their self-concepts; to their identities. Bullying is an attempt to instill fear and self-loathing. Being the repetitive target of bullying damages your ability to view yourself as a desirable, capable and effective individual.

"There are two ugly outcomes that stem from learning to view yourself as a less than desirable, incapable individual. The first ugly outcome is that it becomes more likely that you will become increasingly susceptible to becoming depressed and/or angry and/or bitter. Being bullied teaches you that you are undesirable, that you are not safe in the world, and (when it is dished out by forces that are physically superior to yourself) that you are relatively powerless to defend yourself. When you are forced, again and again, to contemplate your relative lack of control over the bullying process, you are being set up for Learned Helplessness (e.g., where you come to believe that you can't do anything to change your ugly situation even if that isn't true), which in turn sets you up for hopelessness and depression.

"At the same time, you may be learning that you are helpless and hopeless, you are also learning how you are seen by bullies, which is to say, you are learning that you are seen by others as weak, pathetic, and a loser. And, by virtue of the way that identity tends to work, you are being set up to believe that these things the bullies are saying about you are true."

Mark Dombeck's above observations remind me of a powerful idea that Peter J. Ferguson wrote in his book *How to Love Yourself:* "It is not yourself you hate! It is the things you have come to believe about yourself. But those thoughts didn't originate from you."

Where do the thoughts originate? From bullies, including Opportunists and Guilters!

When there is no opinion, there is no suffering; where there is no judgment, there is no pain. —Marcus Aurelius

My point here is that Opportunists and Guilters *impose their judgmental opinions* on their followers and thereby create great pain. So let's discuss *Countermeasures* to the methods that create self-loathing.

a) Guard the entrance to your mind.

Let's begin with this quote:

Man is made by his belief. As he believes, so he is. —Johann Wolfgang von Goethe

If you believe, as some spiritual paths emphasize, that you're broken and living in exile, what is the logical outcome of that? For the people I talked with who do believe this, I have seen some serious consequences. A number of individuals I have met of the "broken and in exile" crowd are among the most physically fragile and sickliest people I know.

There are a number of research studies that seek to find a connection between how people think and how this manifests in their bodies. In fact, psychoneuroimmunology is described as the study of the interaction between psychological processes and the nervous and immune systems of the human body. Authors Linda Brannon and Jess Feist noted that the majority of research in psychoneuroimmunology has "focused on the relationship between various stressors and altered immune system function." (*6)

Imagine the pressure a person feels when burdened by great feelings of guilt and fear that some form of punishment from God will be excruciating and eternal.

A number of studies show the connection between emotional stress and intense effects on the body. For example, a number of reports reveal abundant evidence that severe and acute emotional stress following an earthquake or other natural disaster or the loss of a loved one can result in hypertension, a heart attack or sudden death (the research of P.J. Rosch). (*7)

Perhaps you've noticed the pressure the Opportunists and Guilters exert over their followers: the constant hammering of fixed ideas and emphasis on guilt. Followers often report that they feel that "they're never good enough."

On the other hand, the people I know who feel that they have a loving connection with Higher Power are the ones with more hope and better health.

When I say, "guard the entrance to your mind," I mean: pay close attention to what you watch, read, listen to (as in songs, radio news, talk shows) and see on TV and in films. Are you giving yourself a steady diet of doom and gloom? Are you constantly visiting websites that emphasize that human beings will tear this world apart? Or do you seek to take in balanced input? That is, are you viewing more than warnings of disasters and potential disasters? Do you make sure to view positive messages about the good things that people are doing, too?

Be sure to partake of positive influences in the form of books, audio programs and even the comments of notable, positive people.

Sometimes a dream just whispers. . . . The hardest thing to listen to is your instincts. Your personal human intuition always whispers. It never shouts. You have to, every day of your lives, listen to the whisper . . . If you can listen to the whisper and it tickles your heart and it's something you think you want to do for the rest of your life, then that is what you will do for the rest of your life. And, we will all benefit from everything you do.
—Steven Spielberg

Some people who make sure to gain adequate nutrition for their bodies fail to get positive "nutrition" for their minds. But this is *not* for you. Take care of yourself.

Realize that even though a Guilter is a devout person, he or she may sincerely want you to hate yourself (self-loathing) so that you will come to God. On the other hand, I recall a friend who said, "I learned that the *Gospel of John* includes the passage 'God is love.' And I thought, 'If that's true, God's love would be a higher level than the conditional love my mother shows me.'"

God, to my friend, is a Being of unconditional love.

It is up to you, if you have a spiritual path focusing on God, to choose which interpretation of God you feel *will empower you to lead a productive and enjoyable life.*

b) Practice earning your own approval.

"Others' approval is like an occasional dessert," is an idea that I've written into a number of my books, including *10 Seconds to Wealth*. It means a lot to me because I've experienced the futility of seeking certain people's approval.

When I say "certain people," I'm acknowledging that some people simply do *not* give approval. You cannot earn it. Or the cost of conforming to their ideal would deprive you of your own unique identity. For example, some of my friends simply do not like my writing in my business books. Fortunately, I don't let that slow me down.

So let's shift gears. Here's a helpful question: How do you earn you own approval? Start small. Set a small goal, take action and fulfill that goal.

Here is an example of how I earned my *own* approval. One of my goals is to be supportive of friends. A friend said that she wanted to make a certain documentary film. Now I know that her heart's desire is to direct narrative feature films. But she was talking about directing a small documentary film. I wanted to be supportive so *I restrained myself from offering advice*. I did NOT say, "Wait a minute. You told me you want to direct narrative feature films. A documentary is not on that path."

Instead, to be supportive, I said, "It sounds like you'd really enjoy making that documentary."

So by restraining my initial reflex to offer advice, I did something valuable *in my own eyes*. I was supportive. I did not let my first thought escape my lips. My point is that we *can* approve of ourselves as we take action to support our real personal goals. How does this counter the Opportunists' and Guilters' efforts to get people to feel self-loathing? When you support your own goals, you are not waiting for someone else's approval. You are less vulnerable.

c) Develop your Three Levels of Goals.

To counteract the efforts of Opportunists and Guilters who encourage self-loathing, take control of your life. How? Through your well-chosen goals. When you focus on your own dreams and goals, you are providing yourself with direction.

Human beings are often goal-seeking creatures. If you don't provide yourself with direction, an Opportunist or Guilter will rush in to fill that void of lack of self-leadership. Don't let that happen. Why not? As I mentioned earlier, only *your own* intuition will guide you on your personal and unique path.

Devote time to find your *own* goals. If you ask a number of people what their goals are, they might say: "Oh. Well . . . I'd like to earn some more money. Maybe, get a nicer car someday . . ." This may be useful or not. But one thing we see is a vagueness present. *Truly motivating goals are specific.*

Instead, it's helpful to develop a specific set of goals along these lines:

a) *Dark Boot Goals,*
b) *Golden Pull Goals, and*
c) *Green Tranquility Goals.*

I call these the "D.G.G. Goals."

Dark Boot Goals

Many of us tend to live mostly in Dark Boot Goals. I call them "dark boot goals" because they metaphorically kick us to do certain actions like pay bills and do tax paperwork. Some people call these "maintenance goals" and they're not fun. They are the "I have to do this" parts of life. Some of my friends complain bitterly that their lives are stuck in this drudgery area of life. When I'm in their presence, I listen compassionately. But I wish that they would *move onto* Golden Pull Goals.

Golden Pull Goals

Here is where the fun, excitement and joy of life arises. These are goals that are enticing; they pull you forward toward them. If you're a musician and you're thinking of recording a song, that's a Golden Pull Goal. If you're getting married, you and your spouse-to-be are probably immersed in the planning and taking action to create a dream wedding. I attended a wedding recently—what a marvelous, hopeful event. Here are two people saying: "I will stand by you in good times and times of strife. You can count on me." What excellent Golden Pull Goals. My sweetheart and I have enjoyed 11 years together. Each day, we make the loving choices to listen to each other and support each other. When people make a commitment to Golden Pull Goals, they experience a different form of freedom. Different from what? Different from an aimless bouncing from one pleasure to another. With commitment, it is like you are jumping onto a whole new path with new opportunities for joy. What kind of new path? You could start a business, get married, or have children. All of these paths have tough components, but they also have joyful moments, too. In my first book (which eventually blossomed into *10 Seconds to Wealth*), I wrote about "freedom through commitment."

To support your Golden Pull Goals, be careful about your habitual thoughts. Some habitual thoughts can drain you of energy and paralyze you. For example, some new business owners say, "I don't like to sell. Marketing makes me feel bad." Having observed that disempowering attitude in clients and audience members, I grew concerned and wanted to do something to help business owners get the word out about what they offer. So I wrote a book *Full Strength Marketing* (co-authored with Linda L. Chappo). And I wrote my strategies for an empowered, positive approach to marketing. When discussing the methods of the book, I often say, "You're sharing, not pushing."

Along the lines of "You're sharing, not pushing"—Do you see the power of simply shifting your thoughts and how you approach a situation? You gain two things: a) a well-spring of energy and b) marching orders of positive things to do. How so? Everything we do begins with a thought. If you begin with "I hate this," you're likely to shut down emotionally. Contrast that with, "I want to find some way to share what I do in a way that I enjoy." Do see how one thought can start a positive series of thoughts? From there you can make a positive action plan. Take action to fulfill your dreams. This is an essential component of Golden Pull Goals.

Golden Pull Goals fill you up with positive energy, whether you're making a dream come true or marketing your own business—or both.

When you develop your Golden Pull Goals, consider that only focusing on career-related goals can be a problem. In the article "Top 5 Regrets of the Dying," author Bronnie Ware noted that the most common regret of the dying was: *"I wish I'd had the courage to live a life true to myself, not the life others expected of me."* And the second most common regret was *"I wish I didn't work so hard."*

The other regrets of the dying, expressed in Bronnie Ware's article, were:
"3. I wish I'd had the courage to express my feelings.
4. I wish I had stayed in touch with my friends.
5. I wish that I had let myself be happier."

My point here is that when we list our own Golden Pull Goals, it would be helpful to take the 5 Regrets of the Dying into our thoughts and make sure that we are daily taking action to avoid such painful regrets. For example, you could turn around the regrets into your goals for life. Here are examples:

1. Every day, I demonstrate the courage to live a life true to myself, not the life others expected of me.
2. I make sure to enjoy my life on a daily basis and avoid only working hard. I learn to work smart.
3. Daily, I demonstrate the courage to express my feelings.
4. Each day, I contact two friends.
5. Each day, I think about what brings me happiness and I do something in that direction.

One might view the above statements as affirmations, which I have mentioned are present-tense, positive and personal statements. So it might help to get more specific. Here is another version of the list.

1. Every day, I do two things that are a stretch for me, whether it is making the tough phone call or working on a project that only I see the value of.
2. Every day, I watch something funny on video to be sure I enjoy laughing.
3. Daily, I demonstrate the courage to express my feelings. I express a kind comment to two people each day.
4. Each day, I contact two friends.
5. Each day, I pause for five minutes and look at my list of what makes me happy. I do something (even for just 10 minutes) from that list.

Green Tranquility Goals

Green Tranquility Goals are about peaceful "being." Some of us happen upon these goals after hitting burnout with the above Dark Boot and Golden Pull Goals. As a number of authors have noted, we are human beings and not merely "human doings."

In coming up with the name Green Tranquility Goals, I chose the color green to symbolize growing and blossoming. Human beings can blossom, too!

Here are examples of Green Tranquility Goals:
- I meditate each day.
- I have quiet time for prayer each day.
- I read spiritual material each day.
- I exercise daily.
- I devote focused time to talking with and listening to my spouse each day.

The spiritual is the parent of the practical. — Thomas Carlyle

A person who walks through life with inner peace has a reservoir of patience and energy to apply to the tough situations of life.

Let's face it. So many of us get completely enmeshed in just keeping up with the demands of work. I can relate. Sometimes, I work a portion of each day of the week. Focusing so much on work can make it easy to get caught in the trap of thinking more money equals more fun and goodies. How? It's like a person thinks: "I work so hard. I deserve a better car and house, and more exotic vacations." How does one fund such plans? By working more, getting promoted and working more. Wait a minute. Let's look at another view:

Real wealth is discretionary time. Money is merely fuel for that wealth. — Alan Weiss

So I invite you to develop your own Green Tranquility Goals so that you enjoy and make a priority of having discretionary time to "just be" and "just be happy."

Remember, the three above types of goals help you take control of your own life. This is crucial so you don't, by default, give some measure of control to an Opportunist or Guilter.

Focus on Dark Boot Goals, Golden Pull Goals and Green Tranquility Goals. This brings high productivity, success and fulfillment to your daily life.

Point to Remember:

Opportunists and Guilters encourage self-loathing so you're in so much pain that you're desperate for their "salve."

Your Countermeasure:

Develop your own good feelings about yourself and your life by setting Dark Boot Goals, Golden Pull Goals, and Green Tranquility Goals. Then take action.

DARK SEDUCER'S METHOD #3: DENY YOUR INTUITION
(6 Dark Seducer's Methods)

How does an Opportunist or Guilter get a person to deny his or her own intuition?

Here are examples of language that an Opportunist or Guilter uses:

"No matter what you feel, you must realize this scripture is from God. This is how you must live to be holy. If you fail do these things, you have no way to enter Heaven."

or

"We are united by our beliefs. And this is what we believe..."

Opportunists and Guilters want to make belief more important than *your inner knowing* or intuition. Emphasizing beliefs (they provide) calls into question the validity and usefulness of one's *own* intuition.

Every time you don't follow your inner guidance, you feel a loss of energy, loss of power, a sense of spiritual deadness. —Shakti Gawain

The Opportunist loves it when you feel some spiritual deadness. Why? Because they want to be someone you cling to. (And then they'll later ask for money.)

Your Intuition vs. Someone Told You a Story

I could not say I believe—I know! I have had the experience of being gripped by something that is stronger than myself, something that people call God. —Carl Jung

Carl Jung reports above that he had a personal experience; this is different than merely accepting some story that another person told you.

Truth stands, even if there be no public support. It is self-sustained. —Mahatma Gandhi

Let's Talk about Belief
In my teenage years, my father repeatedly threatened me with sending me to juvenile hall. This threat was unjustified in that I was a model student at a college preparatory high school and did not have difficulties with drugs or alcohol.

So I believed him and his threats. He was my father.

Then when I was 35 years old, my father laughed while he told me that he never intended to send me to juvenile hall.

I had *believed* my father's lies. Yes, my father laughed as he told me about his lying tactics. He did *not* see the harm of his tactics and he revealed (yet again) that he had no thought or care about pain he caused.

So the above is an example of how a person can believe something that is false and which does him no good.

Belief is such a powerful thing—but because it is, it can also be very destructive and it's very easily manipulated.—Jena Malone

I invite you to look at your beliefs. Are they now your beliefs? Were they merely beliefs that you ingested with your childhood's apple juice or milk? What do you want to believe now?

Faith is much better than belief. Belief is when someone else does the thinking.—R. Buckminster Fuller

This is a powerful distinction. I had a belief that my father's threat was real.

The constant assertion of belief is an indication of fear.
—Jiddu Krishnamurti

When an Opportunist or Guilter tells a person what to believe, they exert power over that person. Be careful about such a situation. You need to provide leadership for yourself. (Opportunists and Guilters are happy to assume the reins of leadership over as many people as possible.)

On the other hand, a Spiritual Leader can help you harness the positive power of nourishing beliefs. In addition, some people are momentarily gifted with nourishing ideas. (I'll leave it to you, the reader, to decide who you think is a Spiritual Leader.)

Here are some helpful thoughts on beliefs:

The thing always happens that you really believe in; and the belief in a thing makes it happen. —Frank Lloyd Wright

These then are my last words to you. Be not afraid of life. Believe that life is worth living and your belief will help create the fact. —William James

And above all things, never think that you're not good enough yourself. A [person] should never think that. My belief is that in life people will take you at your own reckoning. —Isaac Asimov

a) Make space for your intuition.
You need to deliberately make space for your intuition. Why? A Guilter will make efforts to spoon feed you his or her ideas all the while attempting to scare you that you must follow or get condemned for eternity. Often, such spoon-fed beliefs take up the space both in your consciousness and your subconscious mind.

Belief gets in the way of learning. —Jeremy Collier

I have seen this with some people at parties. They hold certain extreme beliefs and then they cut off other people's conversation. If one does not give space for intuition or listening to another human being, there is no possibility for learning something new. Without the ability to learn something, often a person cannot take new action. People remain stuck in ruts.

To break out of a rut, you need access to your intuition. One way to make space for your intuition is to realize the difference between the "voice of intuition" and the "voice of fear."

- Your intuition is the voice of "expand, experiment, take an appropriate risk."
- Fear is the voice of "contract, hide, do nothing."

Always be yourself, express yourself, have faith in yourself, do not go out and look for a successful personality and duplicate it.
—Bruce Lee

Opportunists and Guilters promote the idea that all truth is outside of you and that you must be told stories and led by them. Opportunists and Guilters expect you to believe what they tell you to believe. A horrible, extreme example was when Jim Jones told his followers in Jonestown to drink Kool-Aid laced with poison so they would all go to a better world. This is a tragic example. And I submit that it is also tragic for people to live in pain and divine terror even if an Opportunist or Guilter is not requiring suicide.

I'm not in this world to live up to your expectations and you're not in this world to live up to mine. —Bruce Lee

b) Observe where you feel your intuitive feeling.

Where do you feel your intuitive feelings? In your gut? In your chest?

Our intuition is a source of information beyond our rational mind. The challenge for many of us is that we don't stop and listen to our intuition.

The less effort, the faster and more powerful you will be. —Bruce Lee

Bruce Lee wrote about using the physical body for martial arts movements, but his comment also applies to our experience or lack of experience with our intuition. In martial arts, if you're tense or you tighten up, you create resistance for yourself. I know this personally, having studied karate, gung fu, judo and tai chi. When you resist, you're slower and clumsy. Similarly, if you tighten up your approach to life by staying stuck in your head (just thinking with your rational mind), you'll stop yourself from flowing with the universe and receiving empowering insights.

On the other hand, a Zen Buddhist will meditate, or flow in the moment, often welcoming *satori*, that is, a sudden flash of insight. For some forms of meditation, the meditator simply sits down, just observes his or her breath flowing in and out on its own accord.

So to receive an intuitive flash of insight, we find that we often need to pause. Relax. Exert less effort. And observe how the intuitive feeling manifests.

c) Provide leadership for yourself and then intuition will support you.

In the absence of you providing leadership for yourself, leadership will still happen. Someone else will be happy to lead you.

Intuition is ready to serve your goals if you point intuition in a good direction. For example, if I want to be more active with filmmaking, my intuition will bring new ideas into my consciousness. I'll even get new ideas as I dream.

You can't hit a target that you don't have. So listen to yourself. Observe what brings joy to you. Set your course in that direction.

Remember, your intuition is the voice of "expand, experiment, take an appropriate risk."

On the other hand, fear is the voice of "contract, hide, do nothing."

Choose which "voice" you listen to.

Point to Remember:

Your intuition is the voice of "expand, experiment, take an appropriate risk." On the other hand, fear is the voice of "contract, hide, do nothing."

Your Countermeasure:

Make space for your intuition and take appropriate action.

DARK SEDUCER'S METHOD #4: UNDERMINE YOUR ABILITY TO HOLD TWO OPPOSING THOUGHTS
(6 Dark Seducer's Methods)

The test of a first-rate intelligence is the ability to hold two opposed ideas in the mind at the same time, and still retain the ability to function. —F. Scott Fitzgerald

How does an Opportunist or Guilter get a person to clamp their mind shut and lose the ability to hold two opposing thoughts? They keep hammering away with just *one* slanted idea or perspective.

Opportunists and Guilters emphasize that their beliefs are true and better than all others.

You'll hear words like: "Our scripture is the *only* one that comes from . . ."

or

"Only by following the words of _____ can you enter heaven."

Why is it a problem when the Opportunist undermines your ability to hold two opposing thoughts? If you swallow someone else's "truth," you will be constrained into thinking that there is only one right answer and you're one of the few who has it. Then everyone else is wrong and that creates trouble. It severs your connection to other people. They are likely to feel that you're looking down on them. You can't get cooperation from someone who feels your disdain. Instead of falling for the Opportunist's beliefs, use these *countermeasures*.

a) Look for two opposing thoughts and think "I can hold these two ideas in mind. I don't need to judge in this moment."

Researchers note that human beings retain traits that ensured survival of the species over the centuries. One ever-present trait is judging in an instant whether something was harmful. This trait still serves us now. For example, I saw a video in which someone instantly judged that he needed to jump out of the way of a car careening into a gas station's convenience store. That instant judgment saved his life.

On the other hand, our instant reaction to judge can cut us off from other people. We do not even fully hear them before the instant-judging kicks in. Instead, pause. Tell you yourself "I can hold two ideas in mind. I don't need to judge this now. I'll do some listening."

b) Pause and think "I don't run that show."

I recall hearing someone asking a friend, "Who elected you king of the universe?" Don't seek that office of "king" or "queen." Why? The problem is: if we think that we are responsible for everything, then an overwhelming number of things become a *threat* to our plans. How? We're going with our judgments about what we think is "right" or how things "should" go.

I'm not sure about your experiences, but I know that I have been off about the nature of events in my own life. For example, the breakup of my first romantic relationship was a tragedy to me at 18 years old. But at 19, I realized that it was a blessing!

So I invite you to give yourself (and other people) a break. Tell yourself, "I don't run that show"—when it is appropriate.

c) Think "it's okay to disagree."

In my Comparative Religion college class, I say, "I won't ask any of you to identify your spiritual path or if you have one. In the groups, during the discussions, no one has to agree with anybody. We're just tossing ideas onto the table."

I point out to the class members that when one is in a religion it is like standing in an equation.

When you stand in the middle of an equation, let's say:

$$2 + 2 = 4$$

everything is logical. Everything makes sense.

However, if someone is standing outside the equation it does not do much good to try to drag them to your way of thinking.

Also, there are other equations like: $3 + 1 = 4$.

You may notice that you get to the same place "4."

So we get to the perspective where "it's okay to disagree."

The person who can hold two opposing thoughts in mind has the capacity to "allow" other people to be as they are. This person can demonstrate compassion and patience. Now that is positive spirituality.

Point to Remember:

The person who can hold two opposing thoughts in mind has the capacity to "allow" other people to be as they are. This person can demonstrate compassion and patience.

Your Countermeasure:

When someone is hammering at you, insisting that only they have the truth, remind yourself that you have the ability to hold two opposing thoughts in your mind. Remember, you do not have to stay in a place of judgment. You can do some listening to multiple sides first. Then you can find your own way.

DARK SEDUCER'S METHOD #5: COMFORT YOU WITH "FRIENDS"
(6 Dark Seducer's Methods)

How does an Opportunist or Guilter get a person to join his or her group? Journalists report about a typical scenario. A new person steps into the religious organization's building. She is tentative. She looks about the interior with a mixture of hope and trepidation. Then, a representative of the Opportunist steps forward. Sometimes a "mother figure" or "sexy person" is sent to engage the new person with conversation.

To a lonely person, an appealing acquaintance is like a lifeline. The lonely person craves friendship. When I think of friendship, these quotes come to mind:

A real friend is one who walks in when the rest of the world walks out. — Walter Winchell

A friend is someone who knows the song in your heart and can sing it back to you when you have forgotten the words.
—Bernard Meltzer

My point is that a true friend will *allow you to be yourself* even if you disagree with him or her.

It takes a lot of effort to nurture friendships, and sometimes people allow all their friends to be from only one particular group. The problem is that any group has "norms"—spoken and unspoken "rules" as to what is appropriate action and beliefs. Richard H. Thaler, director of the Center for Decision Research at the University of Chicago, and Cass R. Sunstein, a Harvard law professor, combined their talents to write *Nudge: Improving Decisions About Health, Wealth and Happiness*. In that book, they wrote about how the state of Illinois used "existing norms" to press more people to choose to designate themselves as organ donors (upon their deaths). Thaler and Sunstein wrote: "People like to do what most people think it is right to do; recall too that people like to do what most people actually do [and] people often do what they believe is right in part because they know that other people will actually see them doing what they believe is right. The same might well be true for organ donations."

My point here is that when all your friends belong to the same organization, the organization dictates "what is right." On the other hand, you have more freedom when you have multiple friends with different groups of reference. You can express different sides of yourself with people of varied backgrounds. You will be free of the fear of losing all your friends if you choose actions outside of "the norms" of one group.

a) Cultivate friends outside the religious organization.

I have a varied circle of friends. Some are far to either side in politics; some are devout and others are atheists. I have noticed that a couple of my friends have become more "brittle" in recent years. They claim that only select websites "have the truth." They talk with few people and predominantly those who agree with them. On the other hand,

when you have multiple friends with diverse opinions and backgrounds, your consciousness can be expanded by the varying points of view. In fact, this is one of the reasons that I read up to 85 books in one year. I want to have various opinions and perspectives in my thoughts.

One reason that it's important to cultivate friends outside the religious organization is because of how people's behavior and thoughts are shaped by their friends.

You are the average of the five people you spend the most time with. —Jim Rohn

Take a moment to think about those five people in your life.

Personal Wellness and Lifestyle Coach Kellie Hosaka wrote: "Change the five people who influence you the most and who you go to for advice when making decisions."

If all five people are in one religious organization, it is likely that an individual will be locked in on one viewpoint. And that person will be "dissuaded" from expressing something different.

Be sure to cultivate friends outside any one group. Guard yourself from being unduly influenced or coerced.

b) Pay attention and ask yourself: "Are these friends or manipulators pulling me in deeper?"

How do you identify if someone is trying to manipulate you or is becoming a true friend? You watch for patterns. A true friend will accept that you are not his or her clone. The person will still care about you even if you disagree with his or her beliefs. If some people are too uncomfortable with you being "different," those people may use social pressure to get you to conform with their beliefs and demands for your behavior.

Watch out for comments designed to keep you in check:

- "You don't really believe that, do you?"
- "Don't you think we should ask Reverend Smith about that?"
- "That's blasphemy. You need to get your mind out of the gutter."
- "Yes, I imagine that's how you feel at this moment. As you learn more about [the particular religion], I know you'll appreciate the truth of _____, and . . ."

You do not need to voice out loud your opposition to any idea. Just keep your own counsel.

c) Consciously strengthen yourself.

This whole book is devoted to assisting you to strengthen yourself. I know a number of people who do "strength training" (weight lifting). They lift weights to supplement a regimen of walking or running. No one can do the weight lifting for them. They must consciously plan and take action. This means something to me because just this morning, I did some strength training just before getting on a train to travel to the city where I teach Comparative Religion to college students.

Similarly, I invite you to fit in that which strengthens you. Does reading uplifting books strengthen you? Then read a few pages daily. Does visiting a kind relative strengthen you? Then fit that in, too. I have a friend who schedules in time each week to do Celtic dancing. She makes sure to strengthen herself.

Remember an Opportunist wants to make you isolated. Do not let that happen. Instead, strengthen yourself by developing multiple facets of your life. The following quote bears repeating.

To laugh often and much; To win the respect of intelligent people and the affection of children; To earn the appreciation of honest critics and endure the betrayal of false friends; To appreciate beauty, to find the best in others; To leave the world a bit better, whether by a healthy child, a garden patch, or a redeemed social condition; To know even one life has breathed easier because you have lived. This is to have succeeded. —Ralph Waldo Emerson

Point to Remember:
True friends accept that you'll have thoughts and ideas that differ from their own. Be careful of "friends" who push you and don't allow room for varying viewpoints.

Your Countermeasure:
Develop friendships outside of the religious organization.

Tom Marcoux

DARK SEDUCER'S METHOD #6: ELIMINATE YOUR SUPPORT SYSTEM
(6 Dark Seducer's Methods)

An Opportunist often seeks to take away your family and friends as your support group. How? The Opportunist will warn you of horrible consequences if you fall under the sway of "unbelievers." The reports of Charles Manson (who led women to commit horrible murders) note how Manson established himself as a guru in San Francisco's Haight-Ashbury, around the time of 1967's "Summer of Love." He soon had his first group of young followers, most of them female. It is reported that many of the women had left other states to gather in San Francisco. In essence, they had cut off their own support systems (families and previous friends).

Jim Jones was the founder and leader of the Peoples Temple, which is known for the horrible November 18, 1978 mass suicide of 909 Temple members in Jonestown, Guyana. Jonestown members also killed five other people at a nearby airstrip. Jim Jones did the ultimate "eliminate your support system" move: he uprooted his followers from the United

States to settle in Guyana. It is reported that in the summer of 1977, Jones had his Temple members move to Guyana after he learned that reporter Marshall Kilduff's article against Jones' criminal behaviors was to be published in *New West Magazine*. Kilduff's article included testimonies of former Temple members stating that they had been physically, emotionally and sexually abused. Jim Jones named the settlement in Guyana, Jonestown, after himself.

Jonestown is a horrible example of the power of isolation.

On the other hand, we notice that people grow strong when they have a whole support system populated by family and friends.

I got a lot of support from my parents. That's the one thing I always appreciated. They didn't tell me I was being stupid; they told me I was being funny. —Jim Carrey

Now I'll ask you: Who do you have in your life who affirms that you have talent and that you're doing the best you can?

I've always thought that people need to feel good about themselves and I see my role as offering support to them, to provide some light along the way. —Leo Buscaglia

Who is offering you support?

If you're going through a patch of your life in which you have less support, then consider getting a counselor, therapist or personal coach. Sometimes, members of my audiences say that counseling costs too much. At this time, there are graduate schools that provide counseling by a graduate student under the supervision of a licensed therapist. There is a sliding scale that can go as low as $10.00

per hour.

When times are rough, you need someone to talk with. Some research notes that people who report feeling lonely often suffer from depression symptoms and the lack of motivation to improve their lives. It's important to get direct personal support from some kind and compassionate people in your life.

Nobody has ever before asked the nuclear family to live all by itself in a box the way we do. With no relatives, no support, we've put it in an impossible situation. —Margaret Mead

With such a fast-moving culture and people moving to other cities to "follow the jobs," we need to observe the pressure we're under. If you do move to a new city, look into possibly joining a support group or a group that shares your interest in something, perhaps a hobby.

a) Learn to say "no."

One way to eliminate your support system is for the Opportunist or Guilter to monopolize all or most of your discretionary time. Without adequate time, you will not be able to support your friendships and familial relationships outside the religious organization.

To protect your relationships and yourself, you will find times when you need to say 'no' and to offer an explanation.

Let's say you have a new religious friend who invites you to a string of events. You find that you're neglecting other relationships. You decide to say, "No." You can say, "Thanks for thinking of me. I'm already prescheduled at that time or "I already have an appointment at that time."

Perhaps the new friend asks, "Oh. What is it?"

You smile and positively say, "It's personal."

In addition, you need to have preset replies like:
- It's personal.
- I'm not ready to talk about it.
- It involves someone else and I don't talk about other people's personal details.

Then be prepared that you'll probably need to repeat yourself:

"As I said, it's personal."

The new friend may say, "I thought I was your friend."

You can reply: "I hear you. And similar to other people, I share some things and don't share other things. I appreciate when a friend doesn't push me."

In published reports about cults, the "recruiters" gain personal information and then manipulate a new recruit. So it's important that you continue practicing to assert yourself and say "no" when you feel it's appropriate.

b) Use your day planner to schedule ways you support your Circle of Supporters.

This morning before I got on a train I called a friend who had dropped off the grid for a while. I said, "I'm calling to catch up and see that you're okay." She told me that she was overwhelmed with sudden duties in caring for an ailing parent. I listened supportively. And I later realized that without my being proactive and reaching out to her, our friendship would probably die on the vine. So it was up to me to make the effort.

c) Watch out for how "existing norms" push people to make a decision in one way.

In their book *Nudge*, Richard H. Thaler and Cass R. Sunstein discussed "existing norms," that is, research indicates that people who are informed of what action is "normal" tend to follow the crowd.

Thaler and Sunstein wrote, "Recall that people like to do what most people think it is right to do; recall too that people like to do what most people actually do." (*4)

Thaler and Sunstein continued, "In the context of environmental protection, people often do what they believe is right in part because they know that other people will actually see them doing what they believe is right." (*5)

Sometimes an Opportunist or Guilter uses a crowd's approval to get an individual to conform. For example, there are reports about how certain Opportunists have influenced people to think that they were suddenly cured of an affliction. It appears that getting a bunch of applause from the assembled crowd had an influence.

How do you defend yourself from inappropriate influence? You make sure to have more than one reference group, that is, you make sure that you're getting support from different groups. If the only support you get is from a particular organization's members, you might just drift in the direction of the existing norms of that group. Be careful.

Point to Remember:

Make sure you have more than one reference group so that you will not be vulnerable to inappropriate social pressure.

Your Countermeasure:

Use your Day Planner and schedule in time to support your Circle of Supporters. Make phone calls "just to catch up and see how you're doing."

CONCLUSION TO BOOK II: DARKEST SECRETS OF SPIRITUAL SEDUCTION MASTERS (DARK SEDUCER'S METHODS AND YOUR COUNTERMEASURES)

We have covered actual methods that Opportunists and Guilters use to lead people around. Remember, the Dark Seducer's Methods:

S—Submerge your self-esteem.
E—Encourage self-loathing.
D—Deny your intuition.
U—Undermine your ability to hold two opposing thoughts.
C—Comfort you with "friends."
E—Eliminate your support system.

Practice the countermeasures. You must keep yourself healthy and strong.

We'll now move forward to *Book III: How to Strengthen Your Spirit (Tune in to Your Divine Gifts)*.

BOOK III:
HOW TO STRENGTHEN YOUR SPIRIT
(TUNE IN TO YOUR DIVINE GIFTS)

Let's talk about your Divine Gifts. By Divine Gifts, I mean abilities you already possess. As a human being, all of the following are as much a part of you as speech: Love, humility, forgiveness, faith, grace and art. Exploring your divine gifts, you develop some "immunity" to the manipulation of Opportunists and Guilters.

Exploring these can lead to a spiritual life without feeling beholden to any particular organization. Certainly, plenty of people do choose to join such groups. Many find value, community, insight in just that. But maybe feeling beholden isn't a requirement. More importantly, no one should feel helpless without such a group, and benevolent groups don't demand any such thing.

As mentioned earlier, an Opportunist is someone who holds to no real spiritual path; he merely uses the language of religion to exploit. The Guilter is at least sincere, but exactly as toxic. This person is indeed devout, believing that to shred a person's faith in himself and to instill terror of divine punishment is a worthy, even holy act.

Along these lines, a number of religions hold that they possess every possible answer–especially what rules to follow and if one does not follow their rules the result, they say, is horrible pain for eternity. This works for both Opportunists and Guilters. Each spends much of their time terrifying people, making them dependent. For example, let us look at one possible strategy. Someone says, "The only way to heaven is through your relationship with Jesus." Then they continue. First is a list of things Jesus will never forgive (*they* say). Eventually they include acts absolutely everyone has in fact committed. All therefore are damned. Everyone. At the same time, they describe specific actions each Sinner (which is *you* in case anyone wondered) must do in order to beg Jesus for pity. Not justice. Justice means torture—torture you are told is only fair. No, you are begging, groveling, cringing for the undeserved gift of mercy. Not directly to Jesus or God, of course. To God's representative. Guess who? (An Opportunist or Guilter.)

The whole aim of practical politics is to keep the populace alarmed (and hence clamorous to be led to safety) by menacing it with an endless series of hobgoblins, all of them imaginary. —H.L. Mencken

Now imagine connecting with the Divine without having to terrorize yourself. That, you will find, lies at the heart of tuning in to your Divine Gifts.

I first shared these gifts in my book *10 Seconds to Wealth*. We'll use what I call the D.I.V.I.N.E. process:

1. Decide (love)
2. Intuit (humility)
3. Voice (forgiveness)
4. Inspire (faith)
5. Nurture (grace)
6. Express (art)

As an introduction, consider benefits and opportunities of these six Divine Gifts.

1. *Love.* You feel energized and on purpose while expressing love. While sharing love, you feel full of life and connected with people and Higher Power beyond yourself. Life has meaning. You don't need to have a romantic partner in that you can experience love by expressing kindness to people you interact with daily.

2. *Humility.* Listening to new ideas. Not just hearing, actually listening. Simply stated, learning from others, growing by being around them, gaining skills you might not have realized even existed! You value your intuition to guide you along your unique path.

3. *Forgiveness.* The burden lifts. When forgiving—not only others but yourself—the cycle of blame and punishment breaks down. You recover not simply strength and joy but also freedom.

4. *Faith.* You feel supported, no longer alone. You come to an understanding of suffering, and with that you feel a patience with which to face life's hardships.

5. *Grace.* You become open to receiving Divine help. You

go beyond surviving to thriving. You notice that you're blessed on a daily basis. Just recall the times when you were in a situation in which a traffic accident almost happened, but somehow everything turned out well and you and all the nearby drivers were safe. That's a moment in which some of us feel touched by grace. Explore three facets of grace:

a) Grace is unmerited favor from Higher Power.

b) Grace is a grateful approach to every moment.

c) Grace is approaching each moment with elegance and refinement of movement or speech.

6. *Art*. Express yourself, finding joy in that expression. We create literally all the time. With every word, every movement, each thought you're creating the next moment's experience.

DIVINE GIFT #1: DECIDE (LOVE)
(6 Divine Gifts)

To love is to be happy with. —Barry Neil Kaufman

Barry's quote is one of my favorites. Just imagine how we'd all breathe a sigh of relief if our loved ones followed that simple advice. If they would just be happy with us, instead of holding judgments about what "we should be doing." Perhaps you've heard family members say, "You know, you should exercise every other day" or "You should tell your boss that making you stay late every night is unfair."

On the other hand, someone who loves you could say: "This is great. I enjoy just sitting here with you. I'm so proud of you!"

That phrase "I'm so proud of you!" came into my experience in my public speaking class. One of my college students exclaimed it when her friend finished giving a speech. The sheer joy and love she put into those words!

Now imagine yourself giving that same gift. Imagine expressing how happy you are to simply be with your loved one. Now. In this moment.

There is another part of this "To love is to be happy with." Each of us as an individual needs to learn to be happy in ourselves!

The most important thing in life is to learn how to give out love, and to let it come in. —Morrie Schwartz

Expressing and receiving love can have a wonderful side effect—happiness. But we can be prevented from experiencing happiness by an addiction to proving ourselves right. We miss out just taking a breath and being happy in the moment.

Love is saying "I feel differently," instead of "You're wrong." —Anonymous

Love is a decision . . . it is a promise. If love were only a feeling, there would be no basis for the promise to love each other forever. A feeling comes and it may go. —Erich Fromm

With love as a decision, what are we deciding? We're devoted to:

a) Quiet our instant judgments about what our loved one "should do."

b) Listen so well that our beloved feels heard.

c) Devote time each day to simply connect with our loved one—without expectations and requirements.

You might look at the above and say, "That's a lot of work." Yes. It does take effort. Begin with a new framework.

Consider the phrase "to love is to be happy with." Ultimately, this phrase becomes an invitation to practice kindness. Kindness to one's self so you have a wellspring of positive energy. And kindness to others. Finally, kindness towards your loved one.

The FreeDictionary.com defines *kindness* as "the quality of being warmhearted and considerate and humane and sympathetic . . . or a considerate or helpful act."

> *Kindness is the indispensable virtue from which most of the others flow, the wellspring of our happiness.... Under its umbrella, kindness shelters a variety of highly valued and easily recognizable traits: empathy, generosity, unselfishness, tolerance, acceptance, compassion ... Kindness begets love. — Gordon Livingston, M.D.*

What are the benefits of kindness? First, true connection with your beloved. It's a whole different level of communication. A level of "I hear you. You're truly important to me. Your well being is more important than my trying to prove I'm right." A second benefit of kindness? You'll feel happy.

> *If you want other people to be happy, practice compassion.*
> *If you want to be happy, practice compassion. — The Dalai Lama*

How do you nurture kindness? You need to make a shift from the automatic way human beings take in input.

> *Beyond our ideas of right-doing and wrong-doing, there is a field. I'll meet you there. — Rumi*

To get to the place of "to love is to be happy with," you need to reach that metaphorical field beyond judgment. And in this field, you can truly be kind. Why? Because for a moment, you will really be present with your loved one. You'll hear them and know them for *who they are* and *not* your instant judgments and false picture of who they are.

Close-minded judgment is a habit, one many of us have developed. Or have had cultivated. Sadly, organized religion often (not always) does the cultivating. More accurately, the Opportunists and Guilters within organized religion do it. They condition people for instant, sweeping criticism—especially of themselves. Fierce self-criticism makes us more pliable. And it spills over onto those around us, poisoning relationships.

For example, I have a friend who gets instantly annoyed when anyone repeats a personal story. I once asked her about this. What I heard were sweeping criticisms about how it was rude, to her, for someone to subject a listener to the same old stories.

At some point during our conversation, I offered: "I've listened to my father tell some stories ten times. But I considered these ideas: The person talking is *not* the same as they were one month ago. The story may have a new nuance. I'm *not* the same as I was one month ago. Maybe only *now* I can hear something new or deeper in the story. In any case, I'll just be with the person. To love is to *be* happy with."

Her response? "I don't believe that! Repeating a story annoys me! It's just plain rude." And with that she shut down the conversation. Later, upon reflection, I drew a connection between my friend's comments and this quote:

People who are extremely dogmatic and opinionated often adhere to their beliefs as a way of simplifying the world and because they are fearful of uncertainty. —Gordon Livingston, M.D.

In continuing my reflections, I thought, "There must be a different way to live." Soon, I came across the ideas of Ariel and Shya Kane.

One way to access the moment is to truly hear what others are saying. If you listen newly to each individual conversation, the act of listening can shift your life instantaneously. It does this by pulling you into the moment. —Ariel & Shya Kane

Consider this for a moment. What do Ariel and Shya mean by listening "newly"? First, we need to quiet down our own ego. The moment is new. It is not just a rehash of all that has happened before. This is a crucial distinction. Why? Think about it: What do we bring to a conversation? Our past and our instant judgments. We use both to prove how we are "right." We even say, "I know what you're going to say."

It's not true! How? This moment is new. This conversation has never occurred before. Will you meet your loved one in the field beyond our ideas of right-doing and wrong-doing?

How can you do this? One way is to ask gentle questions like: "I'm not sure that I understand. What does ___ mean to you?"

How can this help? Words are just symbols, and since our beloved grew up under different circumstances, they may be using the words to mean things other than what we *think* we're hearing. I have seen this repeatedly with my sweetheart over the recent 11 years. On occasion, I'd ask, "What do you think I mean by ___?" Then, she would tell me her interpretation of what I said. Boom! I realized that I needed to somehow be clearer in conveying my meaning and my intention.

So now it's your turn. Will you aim to listen "newly" to each individual conversation? When you listen newly you have a glorious opportunity to express love. And at some moment, you may observe that you're happy. And your loved one is smiling, too.

Point to Remember:
Focus on the idea that "to love is to be happy with." Seek to listen newly to each individual conversation.

Your Action Step:
Pause. Step away from all the complaints, all the annoying details, anything in fact that seems imperfect with your loved one. Ask yourself: What do I appreciate about this person? What about them makes me smile?

And then, smile.

DIVINE GIFT #2:
INTUIT (HUMILITY)
(6 Divine Gifts)

Human beings tend to instantly judge. At any moment, we're saying to ourselves, "I like this. I don't like that. She makes so much sense, but that guy, he's just plain stupid."

In a way, it takes humility, opening the door for intuition. How? For example, a Zen Buddhist who is meditating seeks to connect with the universe and to receive *satori*, a sudden flash of insight. Another person in prayer may be seeking guidance from Higher Power. Such guidance may arrive as an intuitive feeling to proceed in a certain manner.

It takes humility to seek guidance and not to merely rely on first impressions and first judgments. Some Buddhists talk of two different selves: the ego and your true self. The ego is made of fear and tends to depend on rationalizing. The true self listens and trusts.

Our minds can resemble an aircraft carrier deck. Busy. Crowded. Hectic. Vastly complex. During World War II, things became deadlier and more chaotic than ever when a plane crashed into that bobbing platform in the midst of the ocean. When under stress—rushing against a deadline, dwelling on tasks that need doing, making a series of unrelated decisions one after another—our minds end up just like that.

But when you "intuit," you pause. Make space for your feelings. Your guesses. Your seemingly random notions. Observe where they arrive—in your gut? In the chest?

Many spiritual paths emphasize humility, and this is why. The Christian Bible says: "And whosoever shall exalt himself shall be abased; and he that shall humble himself shall be exalted (Matthew 23:12)." Muslim scholars state that pride is a problem, and submission to the will of Allah (God) is the key to wisdom. The Torah, the holy scripture of Judaism, reads: "Remain in awe of God, serve Him, cling to Him. (Deuteronomy, 10:20)" Opportunists and Guilters will insist this means you are nothing before the Almighty. In truth, this means the exact opposite. The Divine wants to talk to you, give you advice, help you along. Listen to the universe, and you can learn. A lot.

I like to emphasize something I call "healthy humility." That's an awareness that at any given moment our perception might be a little (or a lot) off. Not that you are necessarily wrong. Quite the opposite! All of us get right answers as well as make mistakes—just another part of being human. Healthy humility consists of knowing your place in the universe. Neither above nor below your fellow humans. All of us standing shoulder-to-shoulder with each other.

On the other hand, practitioners of Spiritual Seduction push (as in drugs) what we might as well call "'You-are-worthless' humility." According to this idea every single human being is worse than flawed. We are broken in the mold, diseased from inception, nothing but walking, talking pieces of rancid trash. According to the Opportunists and Guilters our desires are in fact evil. Again, the idea is never to see ourselves as equal to anyone. We, and they, are beneath everything, including contempt.

Instead, it can be helpful to take the view of a person as having both positive tendencies and negative tendencies.

I claim to be a simple individual liable to err like any other fellow mortal. I own, however, that I have humility enough to confess my errors and to retrace my steps. —Mahatma Gandhi

Humility is the foundation of all the other virtues; hence, in the soul in which this virtue does not exist, there cannot be any other virtue except in mere appearance. —Saint Augustine

How can humility be the foundation of all other virtues? Because the humble know they don't have all the answers. They also aren't sure they can personally solve every riddle in life. In a word, they are coachable. What I mean is they listen to feedback and adjust their behaviors, their habits and attitudes. Again, the connection between humility and intuition remains a willingness to listen, really listen—to yourself, your fellow humans, to the universe itself. You avail yourself of quiet time, meditation or prayer.

Humility is attentive patience. —Simone Weil

Meditation is often described as paying attention: observing your own thoughts and letting them float away as if on a stream of water. Allowing uncomfortable thoughts to flow away is part of the process. At the same time, "Don't believe everything you think." They are simply thoughts.

Some true, some distorted. Watch them. Examine them. Turn them around and view them from different angles.

True humility is contentment. —Henri Frederic Amiel

It takes humility to be grateful for what you have. The most dissatisfied people I know fail to appreciate anything in the present. "Life should be better" they say over and over. But the words "Life is good" rarely cross their lips. They blame others for most if not all of life's problems. Friends, co-workers, family, the government, the corporations, the Church, and more.

But the truth? These very blamers are the only constant in their lives. Maybe not every issue can be laid at their feet, but responsibility for handling it certainly does. Think how much happier they—and we—might be if we sought learning from each situation, rather than targets for blame.

What's the benefit of making space for your intuition and living with humility? You live on a higher level of success, love and fulfillment. So find your way for listening to your intuition. Receive guidance and, when appropriate, act on it.

Point to Remember:
Focus on humility and intuition. Make time and space to intuit as well as think. You can do that via meditation, prayer or quiet time. Then demonstrate humility by accepting guidance and then acting on it.

Your Action Step:

Provide yourself with times to slow down and experience a quiet mind. Observe where and when your intuitive feelings manifest. Not only in what space, but where in your body? Demonstrate humility and realize your perception may be incomplete in any given moment. Pause.

DIVINE GIFT #3:
VOICE (FORGIVENESS)
(6 Divine Gifts)

The weak can never forgive. Forgiveness is the attribute of the strong. —Mahatma Gandhi

One time, I mentioned, to a friend, a book cover that addressed "forgiving God." Before, I said one more word, he exclaimed, "That's blasphemy!" He, in essence, ended the conversation. So let's take a spiritual approach and look at what forgiveness can be to a human being. We are not talking about "pardoning" God, for example. We're talking about what you and I can do.

When I appeared on a TV show with Dr. Fred Luskin, co-founder of the Stanford Forgiveness Project, he said, "Forgiveness is ending the cycle of blame and suffering." A human being can address her own thoughts and actions about blame and suffering. This is really about an inside job. You're working on yourself, and it's not about changing other people (or God). *Forgiving takes insightful thought, strength and energy.* Why would you work so hard to develop your ability to forgive?

Forgiveness is a gift you give yourself. —Suzanne Somers

Forgiveness is the giving, and so the receiving, of life.
—George MacDonald

Let's begin with insightful thought. Forgiveness concerns seeing the big picture, not necessarily about pardoning anyone. Seeing the big picture is to look with new eyes of compassion at the whole situation. Now seeing the big picture takes energy and insight! When someone hurts us, our senses are often flooded with pain so it is hard to make the shift. It takes time to see the big picture.

Possible elements of the big picture:

- your pain
- the offender's behavior
- the offender's ignorance
- the offender's pain
- a possible spiritual lesson you could learn
- your own behavior to protect yourself
- something you may want the offender to do to make amends
- a big step for you to demonstrate compassion
- you might even need to testify so that an offender serves prison time
- other elements

This section is entitled "Voice (forgiveness)" and we "give voice" to work our way through forgiveness:

a) Voice your pain to someone safe—a trusted friend, a counselor, or maybe to yourself in the form of a diary or journal.

b) Give voice to compassion. Start with empathy for yourself—forgiving every error, each mistake, all the bad habits formed before life gave you the experience to know better. Don't forget the rest of the world remains your equal. They deserve compassion too. We all do. Pain or ignorance led to many of your mistakes. Exactly the same may have led others to make their own.

c) Use your voice to tell a brand new story, one in which your role ends up neither victim or villain. Instead, figure out how to become the hero.

Here's an example of becoming the hero of your own story. For eleven years, Trudy complained about how her then eleven-year-old brother terrorized her, even held her under water (in a pool) when she was six years old. Now she tells the story a different way. She adds, "That's when I learned that I needed to be strong. I used that to inspire me to ask my parents for karate lessons."

Trudy does not need to "pardon" her brother. He had (and has) his own issues. Callousness in his romantic relationships became a pattern, a habit in his life.

What counts is that Trudy ended the cycle of blame and suffering under her control. She refused to waste time talking endlessly about how her brother hurt her. In the process, she stopped reliving the pain. By not picking at the emotional wound, Trudy let it heal. This process is neither simple nor easy. Trudy found it helpful to work with a counselor.

Years ago, I worked with an author who talked about the "book of her life." She was a psychologist who said that her survival of a sexual assault was in Chapter One of her life and she was now living in Chapter Two. She did not deny that the sexual assault was in the book of her life, but she was *not* allowing it to overwhelm her present. She has found her way to forgiveness (letting go) for herself. By the way, she does not "pardon" the sexual predator. The reason I keep emphasizing the difference between "pardon" and forgiveness is that many of us use the inability to pardon bad actions as a barrier to even consider the forgiveness process. So do *not* begin with pardon. Focus on ending a cycle of blame and suffering *in yourself*. For example, one friend told me that she decided to let go of anger and move on. How is this done?

Ways to End Suffering in Yourself

1) Refuse to talk endlessly about someone else's bad actions.

2) Pick specific times to work through your emotions (Perhaps with a counselor).

3) Stop picking at your emotional wound.

4) Find a way to become the hero of your own story.

5) Find some lesson for your own personal growth.

6) Take personal action for your own well being.

Will all upset thoughts and pain end? I do not know. Each person is different. I do appreciate a line in the film Rabbit Hole in which an older character said, "At some point, it [grief] becomes bearable. It turns into something that you can crawl out from under and . . . carry around like a brick in your pocket." So give yourself some time. The target is for you to lose less time to suffering and feeling helpless. You are not helpless. You can take action. And you can get help, Perhaps with a trusted counselor.

Life is an adventure in forgiveness. —Norman Cousins

When it comes to personal relationships, we sometimes need forgiveness. Again, this is about voicing your desire for forgiveness. Here is an example. Even while giving a speech, I'll set up situations for forgiveness. I once gave a speech and said, "Don't you think we ought to do something to reduce our carbon footprint?" A conservative person I know raised his hand and said, "You said 'ought'. I don't think that's right."

My reply: "I was clumsy with my language. I'll look to avoid using the word 'ought.'"

In this example I neither resisted nor attacked in return. I opened the door for forgiveness and harmony to take place.

Mistakes are always forgivable, if one has the courage to admit them. —Bruce Lee

Saying, "I was clumsy with my language," admitted a mistake. My pledge for greater care with my words acted as a gift, not only to this person but the room as a whole.

And, when making errors at home, I literally voice my desire for forgiveness: "I didn't mean to cause you trouble. I've come up with a plan to avoid that mistake. I'll do ___. Would that work?" And somewhere during the conversation I'll say, "I hope you'll please forgive me when you can."

When you ask for forgiveness, who has the power? The person being asked. More than anything else in life, asking forgiveness feels like a trust exercise. You close your eyes, let yourself fall, and hope. What if they don't catch you? Or refuse to forgive? It takes personal strength to ask. Sometimes, we fail. Life is like that. But—the potential rewards can prove dazzling beyond words.

Harmony and love require forgiveness. Forgiveness makes it possible for your relationship to be free to move forward. I have noted that you can find the letters of "free" among the letters of the word "forgiveness."

Forgiveness and freedom are worth the effort. You become stronger. Often you feel lighter, with more energy.

Point to Remember:

Forgiveness is about seeing the big picture and ending a personal cycle of blame and suffering. We're not talking about "pardoning bad behavior."

Your Action Step:

Take some time to consider who and what behavior you may need to forgive. Consider writing in a personal journal or working with a counselor so that you can go through the forgiveness process and free yourself.

DIVINE GIFT #4: INSPIRE (FAITH)
(6 Divine Gifts)

Of the unknown, Faith is knowing one of two things will happen: There will be something solid to stand on or you will be taught to fly. —Patrick Overton

Recently I attended a wedding. The groom had been a graduate student of mine. As I sat on the lawn surrounded by trees enjoying the pleasant warm day with a gentle breeze, I thought of what courage and faith the bride and groom had. They have no idea what tough times lie ahead. At times they will need forgiveness from each other, even when the heart feels weary. Maybe in their fifth year together or their tenth. Or in six months! But they hold hands and vow to love and honor, for better or for worse. Odds are it'll be both.

If they hold to their faith and believe in the essential kindness and trustworthiness of each other, that approach will help. To believe and to trust is to make love manifest.

Perhaps that relates to what St. Augustine meant with: *"Faith is to believe what you do not see; the reward of this faith is to see what you believe."*

By faith we manifest, we testify, we create the life and world that we would choose. No greater act of courage is ever so common, so simple, so very necessary.

To one who has faith, no explanation is necessary. To one without faith, no explanation is possible. —St. Thomas Aquinas

A man of courage is also full of faith. —Marcus Tullius Cicero

A person of courage toughs it out to fulfill a vision. Such a vision could include many things from learning how to listen well to family members to earning a promotion or even to protect one's family.

You block your dream when you allow your fear to grow bigger than your faith. —Mary Manin Morrissey

Mary's comment brings it all into sharp relief: We choose to live in fear or by faith. Many of us choose both, sooner or later. The real question becomes what we do most, which becomes habit. When you walk or drive or fly, where are you going? Towards something? Or away from something else?

So how do you live by faith? In essence, you inspire yourself. Hence, the title of this section. You find a vision for your life and you move in that direction.

Faith is taking the first step even when you don't see the whole staircase. —Martin Luther King, Jr.

Everyone functions in life by some amount of faith. When you make a turn at a four-way stop, you have faith that other cars will follow the laws. Another level of faith manifests in the pursuit of your dreams.

Just because you can't see it doesn't mean it isn't there. You can't see the future, yet you know it will come; you can't see the air, yet you continue to breathe. —Claire London

A faith is a necessity to a [person]. Woe to him who believes in nothing. —Victor Hugo

Faith holds a vision and moves forward in that direction. Fear is about hiding and protecting yourself.

Faith is not something to grasp, it is a state to grow into. —Mahatma Gandhi

Develop your own journey of faith. You grow into it. Practice at holding a vision, using it to eclipse your fears. Learn to embrace uncertainty. By faith you choose your direction, hold to it, and move forward. In this way, you live each day in such a way as to make joy and fulfillment possible.

Point to Remember:
Faith holds a vision and moves forward in that direction. Fear is about hiding and protecting yourself.

Your Action Step:
Write your answers to these questions. What do you truly want for your life? For your loved ones? What will you devote (time, money, efforts) towards making your dreams

come true? How will you hold a faith in yourself to step forward?

DIVINE GIFT #5:
NURTURE (GRACE)
(6 Divine Gifts)

Grace isn't a little prayer you chant before receiving a meal. It's a way to live. —Jackie Windspear

How do you live in grace?
Let's look at three ideas:
a) Grace is unmerited favor from Higher Power.
b) Grace consists of a grateful approach to every moment.
c) Grace approaches each action with elegance and refinement of movement or speech.

Let's explore each idea.

a) Grace is unmerited favor from Higher Power.
Sarah Ban Breathnach wrote: *"Grace is available for each of us every day—our spiritual daily bread—but we've got to remember to ask for it with a grateful heart and not worry about whether there will be enough for tomorrow."*

In my Comparative Religion college class, I discuss how a number of spiritual paths state that Higher Power grants favor. *The Merriam-Webster Dictionary* defines *favor* as "approving consideration or attention, gracious kindness; also, an act of such kindness, aid, assistance . . . a token of love."

When we look at grace as unmerited favor, we see that it is a gift. We do not earn this gift. Higher Power simply gives grace, as we humbly ask for this gift.

Oh, Great Spirit
Whose voice I hear in the winds, and whose breath gives life to all the world,
Hear me, I am small and weak, I need your strength and wisdom.
Let me walk in beauty and make my eyes ever behold the red and purple sunset.
Make my hands respect the things you have made
and my ears sharp to hear your voice.
Make me wise so that I may understand the things you have taught my people.
Let me learn the lessons you have hidden in every leaf and rock.
I seek strength, not to be greater than my brother, but to fight my greatest enemy — myself.
Make me always ready to come to you with clean hands and straight eyes.
— from a Native American Prayer translated by Lakota Sioux Chief Yellow Lark in 1887

Consider finding a way to ask for grace, perhaps in prayer or meditation.

b) Grace consists of a grateful approach to every moment.

The title of this section refers to "nurture." Merriam-Webster Dictionary defines *nurture* as "1) to supply with nourishment, 2) educate, and 3) to further the development of."

How do you nurture grace in your daily life? Make space for it. Observe when you feel connected to the Divine. Some people report that walking in nature brings them to a peaceful and appreciative state of being.

Grace is connection with the Divine and with the divine spark within you—so that you feel the joy of being alive. —Tom Marcoux

One way to connect with a feeling of pure grace that I have found is by listening to classic orchestrated music by Claude Debussy including Claire De Lune and Reverie. My heart literally soars on the sounds of the violins. Other people find grace in poetry or in a child's smile.

An important level of experiencing grace is to nurture in yourself feelings of gratitude.

Can you see the holiness in those things you take for granted–a paved road or a washing machine? If you concentrate on finding what is good in every situation, you will discover that your life will suddenly be filled with gratitude, a feeling that nurtures the soul. —Rabbi Harold Kushner

One of my editors said, "You need to define grace." My first thought is that grace is too big for mere words. My second thought was: *Grace is a profound feeling of gratitude that so permeates you that you feel indescribable peace and happiness.*

So what do you do with that? Devote moments every day, and often during the day, to *turn your attention to what you're grateful for.*

You say grace before meals. All right. But I say grace before the concert and the opera, and grace before the play and pantomime, and grace before I open a book, and grace before sketching, painting, swimming, fencing, boxing, walking, playing, dancing and grace before I dip the pen in the ink. —G. K. Chesterton

When experiencing grace people say they feel empowered. Doubt in the goodness, kindness and even peace in this universe fades away. Like smoke in the wind. Such a state becomes an oasis from the machinations of Opportunists and Guilters. And better yet, when you experience grace it echoes and continues in your daily life.

c) Grace approaches each action with elegance and refinement of movement or speech.

Many of us have observed the graceful movements of Olympic athletes. You might call that an extraordinary example. The truth is that people every day are doing graceful actions in movement or speech. For example, one day my sweetheart was expressing her pain and disappointment. So I hugged her. Words would not do, but one graceful movement helped.

I'm an educator and professional speaker. There are moments when I experience grace in my words. People have told me that they like my phrase: *Your best work is not the triumph of technique but the purity of purpose.*

And I have found grace with my speech when I have said something supportive, even in the face of someone criticizing me.

Now I ask you, "Have you ever had a moment when you said the kind thing instead of merely attacking in return?" You had a moment of grace.

We can pray to receive the strength to do the graceful action in movement or speech.

In addition, we can practice actions so that we can behave gracefully when under pressure. I know this works because I have trained hundreds of college students, graduate students and clients in how to give speeches and gracefully respond to a mean question. Their phone calls and emails tell me how they have successfully handled tough questions while giving a presentation. So you literally can train to become more graceful.

This section serves to start the conversation about grace. Although it may be difficult to concisely describe grace, the experience is profound.

I have not written about this before. When I was 20 years old, I stood at a bus stop on the corner of 22nd and Mission Streets in San Francisco. I was going to my summer job. A little boy was playing with a toy truck on the sidewalk near the curb's edge. He rolled the truck and it went into the street. Without hesitation, I grabbed the boy, preventing him from stepping into the street. A bus ran over the toy truck, demolishing it. I imagined how the bus could have killed the boy. Only then did his mother look up and see the boy crying about his broken toy. She yelled at me in another language.

Later, I described the experience to a friend.

"Did you feel like a hero?" he asked.

I paused and observed what I really felt. "All I felt was grateful that I didn't hesitate."

I experienced a moment of grace.

Point to Remember:

Recall these ideas:

a) Grace is unmerited favor from Higher Power.

b) Grace consists of a grateful approach to every moment.

c) Grace approaches each action with elegance and refinement of movement or speech.

Your Action Step:

Direct your attention to the moments of grace in your daily life. Focus on grace, speak of grace and remember grace. Write down the moments in a personal journal. Neuro scientists and psychologists (including Rick Hanson and Richard Mendius) note that for a positive event to take root in your long-term memory, you need to focus on the positive event for 10 to 20 seconds.

DIVINE GIFT #6: EXPRESS (ART)
(6 Divine Gifts)

My definition of art contains three elements:
1. Art is made by a human being.
2. Art is created to have an impact, to change someone else.
3. Art is a gift. You can sell the souvenir, the canvas, the recording... but the idea itself is free, and the generosity is a critical part of making art.
By my definition, most art has nothing to do with oil paint or marble. Art is what we're doing when we do our best work.
—Seth Godin

We are all creative. It's an art to listen well to a friend as she unburdens her heart to you. You can be artful in the way you juggle demands and demonstrate your support to family members, co-workers and clients.

Many of us feel that art is only a poem, song, film, painting or another expression. In the fields of both music and film, I have met some extremely frustrated people, musicians who spent *a lot* of money on synthesizers and software, who open a music recording studio. I ask, "Do you book yourself into your own studio to do your music each week?" They reply, "No, I'm too busy recording other people's stuff."

Every time I think about this, it's like being punched in the gut. Imagine artists so completely caught up in making a living they lose (or have lost) a self-expressing life.

If you bring forth what is within you, what you bring forth will save you. If you do not bring forth what is within you, what you do not bring forth will destroy you. —Jesus, the Christ as noted in The Gospel of Thomas

We're invited by Higher Power to bring forth that which is within us. That's the "music" (the creativity) that is inside you. Your creativity is Higher Power's gift to you—to brighten your own life and to share with others.

To go further, I had a discussion with friends about art and its importance in life. They shared a number of ideas. J.R.R. Tolkien called creativity the way we emulate God. One friend's favorite acting teacher called theatre revolutionary—because it aims to turn you the audience into a new person. That is what art is about, redefining reality and sharing experience.

Some art is considered grotesque. Look at the tragedy of *King Lear*. Or how many great paintings portray the death by torture of religious figures. Art does not only brighten life, but deepens it, enriches it, makes it more intense so we can *feel* life.

One friend said, "Art reveals life and deepens our appreciation for it. Art does not shy away from the horrible. Why else are movies like *Silence of the Lambs* or *The Godfather* so popular and universally acclaimed? What's the best *Star Trek* movie? It's *Star Trek: The Wrath of Khan* in which the beloved character Spock *dies.*"

Have you ever thought about "the art of living"? Art is self-expression. Like what? Sharing favorite stories. Or baring your soul, sharing your pain and glory, celebrating maybe the terrors and wonders of staying alive. To fully express yourself, you often need to keep working even when you do not feel like it. I know a number of people who do some writing once in a while, but they're *not* finishing anything. So motivation is important in the *finishing* of artwork. The art of living includes influencing and motivating yourself.

One of the most important goals of this book is helping you feel your true strength. An important facet of that is that you support your own self-esteem. Researchers note that people often feel good self-esteem when they know that they have some form of control and that they can affect positive change in themselves. How is that done? People exert some control when they learn to *motivate themselves* to action. You can't be the artist if you're not doing and *finishing* art!

Along these lines, Dr. Michael V. Pantalon has been training people to motivate themselves and others. He holds that many people take the wrong approach, trying to influence a loved one. People tend to try and sell someone on an idea. Instead, Dr. Pantalon suggests we *help the person discover their own reasons to take action.* He uses the following list of questions:

"1. Why might you change?
2. How ready are you to change—on a scale from 1 to 10, where 1 means 'not ready at all' and 10 means 'totally ready'?

3. Why didn't you pick a lower number?
4. Imagine you've changed. What would the positive outcomes be?
5. Why are those outcomes important to you?
6. What's the next step, if any?"

If we answer these questions, we can motivate ourselves to persevere and to express the art that we're creating with our life.

Now let's apply the above questions to building spiritual strength.

Let's see how one of my clients, "Sam," responded.

1. Why might you change?

Sam: "I want to avoid being pushed around by Opportunists or Guilters because I grew up with overbearing parents who shoved their ideas about God down my throat and my brother's throat. You don't want to be around my brother. He's miserable. I want to feel better. I want to be my own man."

2. How ready are you to change — on a scale from 1 to 10, where 1 means 'not ready at all' and 10 means 'totally ready'?

Sam: "8."

3. Why didn't you pick a lower number?

Sam: "What? Okay, I guess I didn't pick five or six because I've been feeling kind of down lately and I'm desperate enough to want something to get better."

4. Imagine you've changed. What would the positive outcomes be?

Sam: "Maybe, get a girlfriend. I'm afraid my feeling down shows. I guess if I felt better about my life and God, people would feel more comfortable around me."

5. Why are those outcomes important to you?

Sam: "I'd like to stop feeling lonely. Also, I'd like to do better at work. Then I'd have a chance at a raise in salary to help me pay some bills!"

6. What's the next step, if any?

Sam: "I guess, first I probably need to write down a couple of the exercises and practice them."

* * *

Now it's your turn. In your own personal journal, or on a sheet of paper, answer the following questions for yourself. We'll call these questions the "Motivate Yourself Questions":

1. Why might you change?
2. How ready are you to change—on a scale from 1 to 10, where 1 means 'not ready at all' and 10 means 'totally ready'?
3. Why didn't you pick a lower number?
4. Imagine you've changed. What would the positive outcomes be?
5. Why are those outcomes important to you?
6. What's the next step, if any?

My point is that a person who engages with the art of living is making many choices like a painter chooses the composition of a painting.

You are the painter of your life.

I took a risk with this section, as my editors have told me. I could have had only a long intellectual discussion of the facets of art. But I also wanted to include some thoughts on the "art of living." If we don't know how to motivate ourselves to *finish* our art (whatever that may be), then we're going to lose our way.

To dabble your way through life can be unsatisfying as some friends and clients have told me. But dabbling is NOT for you. Fully engage with your life. Motivate yourself and *finish* your art. It bears repeating: you can't be the artist if you're not doing and *finishing* art!

Point to Remember:

The art of living is about expressing yourself; learning to motivate yourself helps you open the door to fully engaging with life.

Your Action Step:

Write down your answers to the "Motivate Yourself Questions." Discover what really matters to you and then take appropriate action.

CONCLUSION TO BOOK III:

Once again, here are benefits and opportunities you have when you connect with your Divine Gifts:

1. *Love.* Sharing love, you feel energized, full of life, connected with people as well as Higher Power. Life has meaning. Nor do you need a romantic partner in order to feel the power of love. Simple kindness is an act of love as potentially powerful as any proposal or love sonnet.

2. *Humility.* Listening to new ideas. Not just hearing, actually listening. Simply stated, learning from others, growing by being around them, gaining skills you might not have realized even existed! In addition, you make space to listen to your intuition.

3. *Forgiveness.* The burden lifts. When forgiving—not only others but yourself—the cycle of blame and punishment ends. You recover not only strength, but also joy and even freedom.

4. *Faith.* You feel supported, no longer alone. You come to an understanding of suffering—your own and others. With that comes a patience you can use to face life's hardships.

5. *Grace.* You become open to receiving Divine help. You go beyond surviving to thriving. You notice that you're blessed on a daily basis.

You explore these ideas:

a) Grace is unmerited favor from Higher Power.

b) Grace consists of a grateful approach to every moment.

c) Grace approaches each action with elegance and refinement of movement or speech.

6. *Art.* Express yourself, finding joy in that expression. We create literally all the time. With every word, every movement, each thought you're creating the next moment's experience.

Now we move forward to *Book IV: More on How to Strengthen Your Spirit (The 10 Topics).*

BOOK IV:
MORE ON HOW TO STRENGTHEN YOUR SPIRIT (THE 10 TOPICS)

I first shared the material in this section at my blog www.BeHeardandBeTrusted.com

I am adding more thoughts to explore daily choices that you can consider. Depending on your choices, you either empower or disempower your own spiritual life.

The Ten Topics:
1) Empower Your Beliefs and Leap Forward
2) Where is the Choice? How You Can Express Your Power
3) The One Detail that Creates Success for You
4) Your Power to Truly Connect with People
5) Uncover Your Charisma; Discover the Power of Gratitude
6) Your True Strength for Success
7) At Last, Handle Worry and Move Forward
8) How to Really Live Your Life
9) How You Can Turn Big Problems Into Big Successes
10) Beware of Friends' Conventional Thinking: Your Success is on YOUR Path

1) Empower Your Beliefs and Leap Forward

Have you ever heard someone say, 'I have no choice'? So what do you believe? Are amazing possibilities open to you? Or do you believe that those opportunities are just for "lucky people"? We'll explore how to get your mind to work so well that you feel the energy to take action when you need to. We'll use the L.I.V.E. process:

L – let go
I – inspire
V – view
E – engage

1. Let go

The most successful people I have interviewed have trained themselves to let go of beliefs that disempower them. Many of these individuals have conditioned themselves to move beyond the beliefs that parents and siblings had about what is possible. Some successful people remember how parents said, "Who do you think you are? You don't have that kind of talent. Just finish getting [an accounting degree] and consider yourself lucky."

Saxophone virtuoso Kenny G said that he got an accounting degree because "there are some things you do for your mother." So he earned that degree, but he did something for himself and with his true gift: he finally performed music in his own unique way, and that's when his later album featuring the musical piece "Songbird" became a huge hit.

I know someone, "George," who frequently says, "I have no choice" about nearly everything. He says, "I have a lousy job, but I gotta go to work. I have no choice." and "I don't like listening to my brother complain. But I got no choice."

Consider dropping this phrase "I have no choice." The truth is, George has choices; he just does not like his choices. Really. He could choose to attend night school toward getting a college degree and a more suitable job. (Many people have made such a choice.) He could say gently to his brother, "I'm feeling tired today. How about we talk about something other than your ex-wife?"

Unlike George, you could take responsibility today and make choices . . . and ultimately you'll arrive at choices that you like.

Let's continue looking at the process of making choices. When asked about some of the bad movies that he starred in, Michael Caine said, "I like to work. I chose the best role available at the time."

To say, "I have no choice" is to disempower yourself. Dr. Martin Seligman coined the phrase "learned helplessness." Seligman and Steve Maier did a study in which dogs were shocked no matter what they did. Eventually, the dogs sat helpless even though they could move and escape the grid where the shocks were being applied. (I really dislike this study.) We realize that the dogs had acquired "learned helplessness." Something similar is when baby elephants are tied to a stake with a thin rope. Later, as fully grown elephants with the power to knock over a bus, they still act as if a flimsy rope has them inextricably bound. They have acquired a form of learned helplessness.

But acquiring learned helplessness is *not* for you. Do *not* let yourself stay in the mindset of "I have no choice." Make the best choice of the options that you have. Or make a new option. How? Find a way to do something in *your* way. For example, I wanted to play the lead role in a feature film. I created an option other than going to many auditions and hoping that someone would bestow an acting role upon me. Instead, I wrote, produced and directed a feature film. When the budget precluded the possibility of hiring a particular actor, my co-producer said, "Why don't you play the role, Tom?" And I did take on the dual work of directing and acting. The option of directing and acting scared me. But I decided to be courageous and take on the dual roles. I made some significant mistakes. And I certainly learned a lot.

2. Inspire

Do you make decisions that inspire you? That is, do you choose something that challenges you and perhaps scares you, but will lead to something exciting or joyful? When talking to top people in various industries (manufacturing, technology, medical equipment), I learned that they take appropriate risks. An appropriate risk is NOT gambling. Some people hear the word "risk" and they immediately shy away.

Instead, an appropriate risk really looks like "the next step" For example, Stephanie trains with a master interior designer, then when her intuition calls for it, she takes her savings and opens her own design firm. It is, to Stephanie, her next step.

Some people are fearful to take the next step. What holds them back? Our beliefs either build us up or tear us down. Do you believe that you can stretch and learn what you need to learn?

Here are inspiring and empowering beliefs:
- I can learn what I need to learn.
- I can adapt to tough situations.
- I can attract effective people to help me improve any project.

3. View

How do you view yourself? Are you a person with options and opportunities? Do you view yourself as a human being on a journey of learning, personal growth and self-expression?

Your view of yourself is crucial.

If you think you can do a thing or think you can't do a thing, you're right. — Henry Ford

You can choose to view yourself as a person who is expanding his or her capacities to love, to be creative, to make a contribution to other people's lives — and to enjoy your own life. Here is something that I have observed. Joyful people spread joy. Miserable people who emphasize that they're martyrs (saying things like "I never take time for myself") spread misery.

Pick an empowering view of yourself and go out and do something kind and helpful.

4. Engage

Engage with your beliefs. That is, reflect on your beliefs. Do they empower you? Are your beliefs really your own or were they planted in your mind (perhaps in your younger years)?

So many times, I'll be at a party or gathering of friends and I hear people simply parrot some words that they may have heard on a news broadcast or some opinion-focused cable TV show. I might be tempted to ask the person to "engage with that belief." I might feel like asking: "Do you even believe that? Have you thought it through?" But I do not ask such questions. I'm there to relax and would rather *avoid* starting a debate.

I invite you to engage with your beliefs. Connect with them. Examine them. Analyze them. And discard the beliefs that do not strengthen you.

Ask yourself:

- Does this belief even belong to me? (Does it come from someone else?)
- Does this belief strengthen me?
- Is this belief a leftover of a time when I was small, young and weak?
- Does this belief encourage self-loathing? Can I instead choose a belief that suggests I can get better and be a kinder, more courageous person?

We must take responsibility for our beliefs. Why? Because they determine how high we go, how much fun we have, and how warm our relationships are.

Belief is the starting point that has given us personal computers, better interactions between people, and even placing a man on the moon.

Choose your beliefs with care.

Some Thoughts on "Empower Your Beliefs and Leap Forward" — and Strengthen Your Spirit

Have you really considered whether your beliefs strengthen your spirit?

Why do you believe what you believe? Do you just accept what your father, mother, or guardian told you when you were a child? Do those childhood beliefs serve you now?

My father has a friend who, years ago, would only give gifts simultaneously — one to the girl and one to the boy. So neither child got to receive "a special time just my own." Now if the girl grew up with the feeling "I'm not special" then she might take a related belief into the rest of her life. She might choose a romantic partner who treated her as "nothing special" so then her relationship would be operating as "business as usual." What I mean is, we adopt patterns when we were children and often recreate them in our adult relationships.

So now I invite you to look at the beliefs that you breathed in as a child. Did you merely accept that you have a Higher Power who "likes to punish"?

Do you believe that you are a wretched soul, deserving punishment?

Does this belief strengthen you?

You do have a choice. How? You can now determine what books you read, what sermons you listen to, which religious organization (if any) you belong to.

You have the power to choose positively on your own behalf.

Choose well and you reduce or eliminate misery.

It's worth it.

* * * * * *

2) Where is the Choice? How You Can Express Your Power

What would help you if you feel stuck? Find the important choice hidden beneath your "paralysis." Then make a good decision. Imagine that this is an "And" universe. Life has tough elements AND we can move in the direction of our dreams.

We'll use the A.N.D. process:

A – Appreciate

N – Note

D – Do something

1. Appreciate

A number of spiritual paths emphasize: "If you don't express appreciation for what you have, you won't attract more good stuff." So we have a choice to find something in the moment to appreciate or allow ourselves to remain stuck in the weeds of complaints. I chose the metaphor of weeds with care. Have you noticed that you don't need to do anything for weeds to sprout in a garden? Weeds rise on their own. It's the same with complaints.

So what is *the Choice?* The Choice occurs in every moment. It's two options: Do nothing and let "weeds" rise up. *Or consciously choose a positive direction for your thoughts.*

For example, Phil had this Choice in the moment:

a) Replay the same tired, disempowering thoughts in his head

OR

b) Consciously switch the direction of his thoughts to what is positive in his life and to what he can do to make things better.

Here's another example:

Many years ago, I worked in a bank. I didn't like the work, but every morning, I had a choice to:

a) Get up and complain to myself about how the work was completely unrelated to my talents and interests

OR

b) Recite my personal *10 Blessings*—things that I was grateful for—while taking my morning shower. I'd tell myself, "I'm grateful for the abundance that this job provides."

I chose "b) Recite my personal *10 Blessings*." It made a big difference. How? By the end of the shower, I felt grateful for the positive components of my life. I was energized to face the day.

Here's a final example.

I have observed two teachers, Randy and Nadine, make different choices.

Randy complained bitterly about having a low wage compared to other professions.

On the other hand, Nadine said, "That is the 'deal' that they have offered; and I said 'yes' to it." She also told me that she is writing her first novel in hopes of supplementing her income—and because she simply enjoys writing a novel.

So now it's up to you. What *choice* will you make in each new moment? Will you default to complaints or will you devote your energy to that which empowers you?

2. Note

When I say, "note" I mean write it down. Take a few notes. Actually see what you're thinking. Think about your life right now. How is it going? Often, my clients write a list of "what's not working."

Instead, write a list of what IS working in your life at the moment.

I do acknowledge if there's some big trouble that you're dealing with, it's truly hard to see what is going on in the periphery. In my Comparative Religion college class, I use this metaphor of one form of meditation. The idea is to sit and observe your thoughts as if they are leaves floating down a stream of water. Let the thoughts float by. Unfortunately, some people pick up one leaf and hold it close to their eyes and then they cannot see anything else.

Instead, you can let the leaf float by, if just for a short time. Even if a serious illness is causing you difficulty, you can make good decisions. For example, Laura Hillenbrand, the author of the bestselling book *Seabiscuit*, has said that her chronic fatigue syndrome difficulties reduce her to only writing two hours a day. And still, she has completed another well-received book entitled *Unbroken: A World War II Story of Survival, Resilience, and Redemption*. This book is 496 pages long.

My point is that she really makes good choices about what she does with her two good writing hours a day.

3. Do something

I write a lot. My friends would laugh at that understatement. For example, at one point, I wrote and pulled together material for a total of 30,000 words in 11 days. How? When I sit down to write (even this section), I don't know exactly what I'll write. But I do something. I do not hesitate.

I simply start writing. No matter how I'm feeling, I write for at least a few minutes. Doing some writing each day helps me travel in the direction of my dreams. For years, I have been investing my efforts and time in writing and improving my skills.

I have some friends who truly don't understand the idea of investing. Sometimes, I wish they could meet Greg Bear who exudes more happy energy than most people that I have met. Greg Bear is the author of science fiction books including *Eon* and *Darwin's Radio*. He told me, "It took about ten years before an audience found one of my books." Greg invested years of writing efforts before he could make a living at the craft.

To me, Greg Bear demonstrates the meaning of the old phrase: "Happiness is something to do, someone to love and something to hope for." Writing is something that he does and during the early years of writing he continued to have something to hope for.

If you're missing one of the three elements (something to do, someone to love and something to hope for): do something!

For example, many years ago, fresh out of college, I was without a girlfriend. To say it in a few words, when you're in college there are lots of people around. It was easier for me to find a suitable girlfriend while I was in college.

But fresh out of college (and yes, before Internet dating websites), I was at a loss. But I did something. I attended a workshop. Two things happened. One: I found someone who became my girlfriend for seven years. Second, in listening to the workshop leader, I discovered: "Hey, I could give a better speech than that!" I went on to get training and have enjoyed speaking in various venues across the United States, including Stanford University.

My life changed when I did something.

I invite you to embrace making good choices (even when you do not like your choices).

Make a choice; make a life.

Some Thoughts on "Where is the Choice? How You Can Express Your Power"—and Strengthen Your Spirit

In every moment, you have a choice to strengthen your spirit or do something else.

Often, as I mentioned, we do not like our choices. So the "easy" thing to do

is to complain. Often complaining is a spiritually crippling choice. How? It puts us into a victim state of being. Really? Yes, when we complain we're often describing someone else as a villain doing something bad to us.

Earlier, I mentioned a teacher who complained about the low wage he has accepted.

Did you notice the important detail?—"he has accepted."

Once we say "yes," the empowering choice is to *acknowledge our choice*. That is, we avoid saying "I had no choice."

In my own life, when I have accepted a contract for a modest sum of money, I chose not to complain about the money. Instead, I said immediately, "I'm grateful for the steady work."

So an important spiritual choice is to focus on gratitude everyday.

Gratitude empowers you; it does make you spiritually stronger.

* * * * * *

3) The One Detail that Creates Success for You

Have you felt that somehow your life is stalled? Or maybe it's like you're trying to drive forward but your car's parking brake is on? To get unstuck, many people try using affirmations, which are personal, positive, present tense sentences like: "I am physically fit and full of energy." There is something that has even more power that an affirmation. What? An empowering question: "Does this strengthen me?"

You can apply the question "Does this strengthen me?" to any action you're considering. You can even apply "Does this strengthen me?" to your beliefs!

Now we'll use the Y.E.S. process:

Y – Yearn for empowering beliefs

E – Energize

S – Surrender (let go)

1. Yearn for empowering beliefs

Submit your beliefs to the question: "Does this strengthen

me?" (Yes, I've mentioned this earlier. And it bears repeating here.) I know a couple of people who believe that they are not lucky. Does that strengthen them? No. In fact, their "poor me" stories drag everyone down.

So look at your beliefs. Do they strengthen you? If not, consider tossing those beliefs into a trash can.

2. Energize

When you submit an action to the question "Does this strengthen me?," you can create positive energy in your life. How? Here's an example. Today, I have a packed schedule with revising a book and grading the work of graduate students. I thought about calling a particular friend "Lyndon." But he's been in an awful mood. So I submit the idea of calling Lyndon to "Does this strengthen me?" Then answer: No! So I have decided to guard my energy and avoid calling him today.

3. Surrender (let go)

Many spiritual paths emphasize the value of "surrendering or letting go." You turn over the situation to a Higher Power . . . or you just let go of your constricting beliefs.

When we pause and think about it, there are many things we do not control (the stock market, the mood of a friend, and more). It's important to recognize what we don't control, and to examine our beliefs. If you hold any belief like: "I cannot be happy if my friend is not happy," you have restricted your positive possibilities.

Therapists and personal coaches learn that they can provide support and listen to a client, *and* not go down into the depths with that person. One can cry for some moments and then shift the direction of one's thoughts.

In addition, you can learn to avoid "rescuing" people. Sometimes, a friend may need to experience trouble to learn the tough lessons. For example, Serena was studying for an important licensing exam. Her friend George called her and said, "I stayed out too late last night, can you get me to my job this morning?" Serena said, in a gentle but firm way, "George, I'm really sad that I can't help this one time. Maybe you could call a cab? I have to go. Take care."

There is an old phrase that goes something like: "You need to take care of yourself so you have the capacity to help others. You cannot give what you don't have."

The truth is: we must let go of a plan to try to be "perfect" and "always there for others."

Some people who try to be perfect seem to think of themselves as "martyrs." They overwhelm themselves by always giving too much. Sometimes, these people come across as really bitter.

Sometimes, we need to let go of trying to do everything. . . and devote time to rejuvenating and restoring ourselves.

Less misery in you means less misery in the world.

An old phrase holds: "Take care of you—for me." When you take care of yourself, you do not need to lean on friends and family so much. Remember to submit your plans and beliefs to this question: "Does this strengthen me?"

Some Thoughts on "The One Detail that Creates Success for You"—and Strengthen Your Spirit

Let's look at "You need to take care of yourself so you have the capacity to help others." Why? Because I've noticed that a number of people seem to leave themselves off their own priority list. This is a serious mistake. Here's the reason: You need nourishment (for your mind, body and spirit) to function well. For example, I tend to write first thing in the morning. This provides me with a personal victory immediately, which nourishes my soul and places a smile on my face.

No matter what challenge arises in my day, I have started well and I can take the warm feelings of my personal victory with me into the rest of the day. So what nourishes you? Would a walk in the morning give you a good start? How about listening to your favorite music? Or reading an empowering book? Ensure that you build your capacity.

* * * * * *

4) Your Power to Truly Connect with People

Have you ever said something like: "I don't understand him. How could he do this to me?" The top successful people I've interviewed have demonstrated keen insights into human behavior. Many of them demonstrate true charisma as they make you feel like you're the most important person in the room. The charismatic person can even find something good in you, although he or she deeply disagrees with you.

The test of a first-rate intelligence is the ability to hold two opposed ideas in mind at the same time and still retain the ability to function. — F. Scott Fitzgerald

This is a really important point. Can you imagine that someone can be your friend and hold intensely different political ideas than you do? It is possible. I have friends who are polar opposites in their political views.

Can you hold the idea that a friend can love you but say something really mean on an off day? What we need is to be able to connect with people even if they're different from us or under some form of stress. So we'll use the H.O.P.E. process to connect with people even if they don't agree with us:

H – Honor the fear
O – Open
P – Perceive
E – Express compassion

1. Honor the fear

I imagine that you may find this phrase "honor the fear" to be strange. Stay with me now. When I look carefully at the faces of people that I have met in different parts of the world (from New York to Nassau; from Indiana to Japan), I see both hope and concern. The concern may flash across the face ever so briefly. My point is: if you can imagine that the person you're talking with is similar to you, someone with fears and joys, you might just extend more compassion toward him or her.

Why does someone believe something? Often if we look closely, we may find fear beneath an opinion. Some people hold an idea because they're afraid of losing their freedom to some situation. At the time of this writing, in the United States, there are extremely vocal individuals who express their anger about whether businesses will be hampered with taxes or whether some individuals will lose medical benefits (among many other issues). Do you see how fear of having something taken away incites anger?

What rules the world? Some people say "greed" or "desire for power." Could it be that a fear of loss is underneath extreme desires for money or power? Perhaps the person obsessed with wealth-building never wants to be vulnerable or a victim again.

When I say "honor the fear," I do *not* mean "agree with

the fear." I'm really talking about compassion. If someone says something in an angry tone, consider asking yourself: "Hmmm. I wonder what this person is afraid of?"

Why? Because this question and related thoughts may help you remain calm. And you may also be able to create a connection as you look upon the person with compassion.

2. Open

Nothing new can happen without some openness. Someone I know talks about her fondness for a comment from Chesterton: "An open mind is like an open mouth, only good to clamp down on something solid."

Hold on a moment here. If the mind clamps down, then nothing new can get in. This was vividly demonstrated one time when I was directing a feature film. Imagine actors gathered together and eating lunch. One actor said, "I've thought that it would be a good idea not to have a TV. Then my children would have to do other things like play outside or get a hobby like painting."

The group of actors was starting to "clamp down" or agree with the idea that no TV in the house was good for children. [Okay, I get it: on some level this might seem ironic—actors and no TV?!]

Then the star of the feature film said, "I lived in a neighborhood where one house had no TV. When the kids went to other children's homes, they didn't play. Magnetically, they were drawn to the TV. It was too big of a deal not to have a TV in the house."

At that point, the actors in this impromptu discussion had their minds "opened to another point of view."

My point is that a form of "groupthink" was going on with everyone agreeing with one idea until the star of the feature film voiced a new idea. On some level, people in the group had not completely "clamped down" on the "no TV" idea.

I invite you to keep your thoughts "open" so that you may learn something new or consider a situation from a new angle. Why? The person who can adapt, who is not rigid, has more chances to succeed.

3. Perceive

The Merriam-Webster Dictionary defines perceive as "to become aware of through the senses."

Here's an important point. As human beings, we often don't have all the information. about a situation. We can be fooled by our own incomplete preconceptions.

Instead, you find that you succeed more often if you perceive that you don't have all the answers in this moment and that your perception could be off.

Look more deeply into whatever situation you find yourself in. You'll find that seeming opposites take place often in life. For example, is it a good idea to limit the TV viewing hours of children? Yes. Is it also a good idea *to not make a big deal* about rationing the amount of TV? Yes. (As we saw above, if the lack of TV is too big a deal, children may be obsessed with the "forbidden fruit" of TV and go to other people's homes merely to watch TV.) Remember, F. Scott Fitzgerald's above comment about the "ability to hold two opposed ideas in mind at the same time." Why? Because using your mind intelligently can help you create a life of more joy and fulfillment.

Holding two opposed ideas is necessary to find the truth, so we can improve whatever situation we find ourselves in.

Here are examples of opposed elements:
- A parent who deeply loves his son but has no idea how to listen effectively.

- A man who expresses his love to his wife by cajoling her to take his advice about what she "should" be doing . . . but he has no idea that his failure to listen is breaking her heart.
- A mother who truly wants the best for her daughter . . . but endlessly criticizes her daughter's actions.

In order for you to go beyond making instant judgments, you need more energy. When you're tired, your viewpoint contracts. To recover your energy, be sure to take care of yourself, gaining enough sleep, good nutrition, exercise, and quiet time. Then you'll be able to perceive that you need more information.

4. Express Compassion

Merriam-Webster dictionary defines *compassion* as "sympathetic consciousness of others' distress together with a desire to alleviate it."

Express compassion for yourself. Get the support you need. If a family member fails to listen to you, find someone else to listen to you, perhaps a trusted friend or a counselor.

Author Joe Vitale wrote: "If you want the planet to be healthy, wealthy, and wise, contribute one healthy, wealthy, and wise person to it." He is referring to you. Misery doesn't just love company. The truth is: misery creates company. Miserable people spread their bad mood around to people near them.

So relieve this world of some misery by being good to yourself. Show compassion toward yourself. Take care of yourself at least like you would treat a good friend visiting your home.

To further you ability to hold two opposing thoughts in mind:

Honor your own fear. Practice "openness" so you can let

new ideas in. Perceive that you don't have all the answers in this moment and that your perception could be off. Then seek to gain more perspectives and knowledge. Why? Because this world needs intelligent, perceptive, humble and kind people.

Now imagine more people doing that. Here comes some hope into the world.

Some Thoughts on "Your Power to Truly Connect with People"—and Strengthen Your Spirit

People dedicated to a spiritual approach to life realize the value in being able to truly connect with people. A number of spiritual paths from Buddhism to Confucianism, from Christianity to Daoism emphasize that it is through our relationships that we do our essential personal growth. How do we learn to be patient and compassionate?—through a relationship.

Relationships are where we practice expressing compassion and kindness. Recently, I had such an opportunity. I was discussing this book, and a friend went for the jugular with this comment: "It sounds like you're a little boy ranting!"

Instead of reacting to his unkind comment, I restrained my emotions. I did *not* take the bait. Calming down the situation, I said something gentle: "You're right. I do have some intense feelings of sadness over the suicide of my friend..."

The seeds of compassion and kindness *are* in you and me. Allow them to bloom. Consider doing belly breathing to calm down. A better world starts with you in this little corner of the world. As Mahatma Gandhi said, "You must be the change you wish to see in this world."

* * * * * *

5) Uncover Your Charisma; Discover the Power of Gratitude

Have you ever felt so tired that you were afraid that you wouldn't feel joyful again? There is something that is crucial, but it takes effort and skill to make it a daily part of your life. It's gratitude. Gratitude can pump you full of good feelings and energize you to make the most of your life. And grateful people exude a form of charisma. Perhaps you've heard someone say something like: "You just feel good being around Susan." To help you develop your own grateful feelings, we'll use the S.A.Y. process.

S – See
A – Acknowledge
Y – Yodel (sing)

1. See

What do you see when you look at your current life? For many of us, the reflex is to see what is missing. Not only do we focus on what we lack, but we also seem to think waiting is okay. I have heard friends say, "I'll feel better when I get the new job." Or "I'll look for a girlfriend when I have a steady job." Well, life doesn't wait for any of us.

I invite you to choose something other than defaulting to seeing what's missing in your life. Instead, go out of your way to see what is working in your life. Emphasize the blessings that you now enjoy. Pull out a sheet of paper and start with these four powerful words: "I am grateful for . . ." Now list all the good things that are in your life.

2. Acknowledge

The next step is to voice your acknowledgement of what is good in your life. In fact, just today, I called up one of my editors and thanked her for helping me be "one of the least frustrated artists I know." What I meant was: I felt safe that she helped me improve the writing so I finished another book. I know good writers who do *not* finish books. They stay frustrated as writers, while I celebrate 22 books up on Amazon.com. And one of my books rose to #1 on Amazon.com's Hot New Releases in Business Life.

So my habit is to acknowledge the great work of my team members. And guess what? As I acknowledge the terrific help I receive, I also feel much better. Acknowledge the kindness and support you enjoy in life. It's a good way to live. You inspire joy in others–and in yourself.

3. Yodel (sing)

"Yodel"—how often do you see this word? I'm including it because it's memorable and amusing. The Merriam-Webster Dictionary defines "yodel" as "to sing by suddenly changing from a natural voice to a falsetto and back." My point is for you to truly feel grateful, it helps to express your joy. Various authors write lines like "then he would shout for joy." I'll add, "Sing for joy."

I recently completed the midterm grading for my graduate and college students. It was really a tiring task. How did I press on? I played music using iTunes. When I was singing, I was happy. I was fully alive.

So sing. Around the time I graduated from college, I was the lead singer of a band. Later, I began my filmmaking career. My point is that I'm grateful for the adventure of being part of a band, and for the later adventure of directing and acting in a feature film. And while making my first feature film, I remember "singing" with my co-producer the phrase: "We're making a movie!" We were singing with joy.

Remember these methods for connecting with gratitude:

S – See

A – Acknowledge

Y – Yodel (sing)

Researchers demonstrate that human beings' experience of life varies depending on what they focus on. Focus on the blessings in your life and you feel better. You'll feel gratitude each day. And you'll become charismatic. And you'll have more to be grateful for. Why? People offer more opportunities to grateful people.

Some Thoughts on Uncover Your Charisma; Discover the Power of Gratitude—and Strengthen Your Spirit

Why is gratitude so important? How you respond to the gifts of life either makes you spiritually strong or not. The spiritually strong person is more resilient. Currently, I have two close friends who are disgusted with their lives. They even admit that they're being negative. What surprises me is that neither person is studying how to be resilient. In fact both are seriously ill. An outside observer might say to them, "You're so negative; you're making yourself sick." I'm not sure if that's true. However, I do limit my exposure to negative people. For what reason? Because I want to keep up my energy levels so I can be kind to family members, friends, graduate students and audiences. Choosing to be grateful and expressing your gratitude about the little gifts in your life is a *True Spiritual Choice*. Make a good choice for you and those near you.

* * * * * *

6) Your True Strength for Success

When was the last time you felt like you were at the end of your rope? To create the success and fulfillment you want, you need to have a powerful combination of self-esteem and humility. We'll use the H.O.W. process:

H – Honor
O – Open
W – Wonder

1. Honor

You need to honor your gifts. One definition of self-esteem (from author Nathaniel Branden) is:

"Self-esteem is the disposition to experience oneself as being competent to cope with the basic challenges of life and of being worthy of happiness. It is confidence in the efficacy of our mind, in our ability to think. By extension, it is confidence in our ability to learn, make appropriate choices and decisions, and respond effectively to change. It is also the experience that success, achievement, fulfillment—happiness—are right and natural for us."

We can think of self-esteem as "fuel." Without fuel, a car cannot get us to a neighboring city.

Some people mistakenly look upon self-esteem as some form of self-obsession. Instead, self-esteem is our belief in our capacity to do well in life. So honor your gifts. Make the most of your talent.

Here's an important point: The person with good self-esteem will "stay in the game." He or she will persist. This person will keep going when all others give up. Why? Because the person with good self-esteem knows that he or she can adapt to whatever comes up in life. The pessimistic person is more likely to give up. Recently, a friend said, "I don't daydream." I felt a stab of pain for my friend. Why? Because he cannot see "more and better." In addition, he doesn't realize that doing something small can lead to something big.

Healthy self-esteem can sustain you through the tough times. For example, another friend self-published a book. A publisher saw the book on Amazon.com and then offered to republish the book in Italian. This publisher paid my friend for the distribution rights in Italy. And a couple of months later, the publisher invited my friend to fly from America to Milan, Italy to give a workshop. The Italian publisher provided the interpreter for the workshop. How did this all happen? It began with my friend having the good self-esteem to finish his book and self-publish it.

My friend also had an added advantage. What? He was aligning his talents and skills with making a positive contribution to humankind. The universe rewarded him with surprising and delightful opportunities.

2. Open

Humility includes openness. For what? To realize that your perception in this moment can be inaccurate. When you demonstrate humility you can learn from every event. This gives you an advantage over a "know-it-all." Someone who is smug or self-satisfied fails to perceive that he or she has more learning to do. Such a person does not seek coaching to improve personal performance. For example, I have some older relatives who are "done with learning." It's sad, actually. Because their days are dreary and repetitive. On the other hand, I'm always looking to learn and explore—so each day is new and fulfilling.

3. Wonder

You need to wonder what you can learn in each situation. Why? The answer is in something Bill Gates said: "Success is a lousy teacher. It seduces smart people into thinking they can't lose."

Instead of being choked by thinking you can't lose, focus on these questions:
- What am I learning here?
- How can we make this better?
- What worked?
- In what areas do I need to make improvements?
- Is there something for which I need coaching?

Self-esteem and humility do not cancel each other out. In fact, they work like partners so that each day you can grow, explore—and experience success and fulfillment.

Some Thoughts on "Your True Strength for Success"—and Strengthen Your Spirit

Humility provides a form of power. What power? A number of spiritual texts invite us to "be like a child." How could that be helpful? A healthy child is *not* complacent like a "know it all" adult. She looks around with wonder. And to a child, just about anything can be a toy. A toilet tissue roll. The Kleenex box.

Imagine that, as adults, we're meant to continue to explore with joy and wonder. I read lots of books. Why? One of the reasons is that I enjoy learning. Humility is part of being coachable. Being coachable is a primary approach of the spiritually strong. Why? Because your options remain open. Think about it. Just how much can you learn? How much can you improve how you listen to a loved one? How much better can you learn to communicate your heartfelt thoughts? There's no limit!

You have a lifetime for making improvements—if you retain humility to learn from each experience. Recently, I felt deep disappointment when a contractor quit a project before it was done. I wrote an email to him: "I have learned much from our interaction . . ." It is true! I have learned better screening techniques in my hiring processes.

So much to learn. The world can be a classroom in which we all learn and play.

* * * * * *

7) At last, Handle Worry and Move Forward

Have you ever worried so much that you felt really drained? Imagine you could deal better with worry and move forward. You can! We'll use a process so you can say "goodbye" to losing many moments to disempowering worry. We'll use the B.Y.E. process

B – Bring light upon the worst
Y – Yield (let go)
E – Experience and limit it

1. Bring light upon the worst

It's the monster in the dark that is scarier than the monster you can see. I have found that if I say out loud the problem that I'm worrying about, it somehow loses some power. Why? One reason is that once I name the problem, my mind automatically starts with questions like:

- How can I handle this situation?
- Who can help me with this?
- What are my resources to devote to this situation?
- What do I need to learn so I can handle this situation?
- What if I try (___), how will that reduce the possible

damage?
- How can I still be okay even if the worst happens?

In many cases, the worst that can happen is still survivable. And when we remember what we've survived in the past, we realize that we have the strengths of adaptability and flexibility. We can build on that!

2. Yield (let go)

The truth is: some things that we worry about we really do not have control over. How is Joe going to feel about this? Do we control that? No. We may have some influence. That is, we may say something in a gentle way. But Joe's feelings and reactions are his own.

So ask yourself: do I really have any control here?

Here are some examples of elements we don't control:

a) the weather
b) someone else's feelings
c) someone else's reactions
d) the economy

My fast way to yield or let go is to say, "I don't run that show." This phrase really works for me because I have been making films and other creative projects since I was nine years old. I'm in my 40's Now and I have had a lot of practice in leading projects.

3. Experience and limit it

My sweetheart and I take a daily walk. Sometimes, she wants to change subjects when I'm talking about a business problem pressing on my thoughts. We have a process. She says, "I'd like to change topics." And I reply, "Okay, you see that street light a block up that way? When we get there, I'll stop talking about this problem."

We came up with this strategy because, in the past, we observed that if I had a few moments to experience my upset and feel heard, I could put a limit on the problem-focused conversation and move on to another topic.

It helps when you give yourself the time and space to feel your feelings . . . then move onward.

When you want to deal effectively with worry, remember:
B – Bring light upon the worst
Y – Yield (let go)
E – Experience and limit it

May you enjoy more positive moments each day.

Some Thoughts on "At Last, Handle Worry and Move Forward" — and Strengthen Your Spirit

It's natural to get concerned about a situation going wrong. Then you have a spiritual choice. Will you hold to a faith that everything ultimately leads to a blessing? When I was a small child, my father would dump a bucket of water on my head and I was afraid I couldn't breathe. I have a made a choice to *not* get bitter about this. And I have used this experience of fear (with a related feeling of betrayal) as fuel for a deep feeling of empathy for my coaching clients, students, readers and audiences. So I choose to identify my deep empathy as, ultimately, a blessing. That is a spiritual choice I invite you to consider now. You can choose to take the view that tough experiences of your life can yield blessings. If you approach life in this way, you can move beyond worry. You can live by faith.

* * * * * *

8) How to Really Live Your Life

Have you ever felt that you were missing something in your life? Sometimes, we find that what is missing from our life is . . . *ourselves*. Are you expressing what is important to you? We'll use the W.I.N. process:

W – Write your life for yourself

I – Inspire

N – Nurture yourself

1. Write your life for yourself

With each decision you make, you are, in essence, *writing your own life*. Write your life for yourself. That is, don't get stuck trying to gain other people's approval. For example, I was at a recent gathering of friends who appreciate feature films. One friend talked about how feature film director Stanley Kubrick won a number of prestigious awards. While I was listening, I had the thought that it was likely that Stanley had more fun making the films than winning the awards.

Among my circle of friends, I know one thing. Each friend does not like some portion of my writing. Some do not like my business writing [those individuals don't like business, anyway]. Some have told me that some of my fiction is too "emo" [emotional] for them.

My point is that while I'd enjoy a friend's approval, I do not base my joy on getting that approval. Which is a good idea, since I have no control over someone's reaction.

What helps me is that I know what my writing is about. My writing is about helping you strengthen yourself.

Although I don't focus on approval as the center of my efforts, I did make a conscious decision to write and release five books on Amazon.com before I finally released my most powerful, intense writing—this book and the two preceding

volumes in the series:
- *Darkest Secrets of Persuasion and Seduction Masters: How to Protect Yourself and Turn the Power to Good*
(an excerpt is available at the end of this book)
- *Darkest Secrets of Negotiation Masters: How to Protect Yourself, Overcome Intimidation, Get Stronger, and Turn the Power to Good*

As I write a book, I enjoy the activity of writing and getting feedback from two editors per book. I like thinking, and making new connections and pulling together research in a vivid, concise form.

Now it's your turn. How could you make decisions based on your heartfelt-focus? Look on approval as an occasional dessert. Don't write your life for others' approval. Honor your own heart.

2. Inspire

The Merriam-Webster Dictionary includes this definition of inspire: "to infuse (as life) by breathing." Do you make conscious choices about what you breathe in? What books do you read? What TV programs do you watch? Do you watch what scares you?

I have talked with a number of people who say that they're "not lucky" or that they won't accomplish the big things in life. My question is: Are they reading books or listening to audio programs that inspire them? Do they read about how ordinary people have accomplished extraordinary things?

Here are two valuable questions:
- What inspires you?
- What have you done today to get a daily dose of inspiration?

3. Nurture yourself

Feed your spirit. What music do you listen to? — angry music or inspiring music?

I invite you to nurture yourself.

Many times, our loved ones will not understand what we're doing, whether it's pursuing a dream or changing jobs.

For example, several years ago, my then-girlfriend saw one of my feature films and said, "I've never seen a movie like this."

Okay. But what does that mean? It could mean that the film just is "not her cup of tea." So it does not work for her.

A number of feature films do not do well at the box office and then find success as a DVD or Blu-ray film. In essence, they find their audience later. Recently, I saw two films that I did not like on first viewing them. They were different from my expectations. But then I realized as I watched them again [watch out for flipping through cable stations!] that now that I knew what they were about I could appreciate them on their terms.

So regardless of when or how a film or other artwork is received, any artist needs to nurture himself or herself. I recently came across the words of controversial comedian Ricky Gervais: "You do your own thing and then you see if you survive. And I wouldn't have it any other way because if you start second-guessing and you're trying to find people who like you or change to make people like you, you're finished. And you're finished as a comedian more than any other thing in the world."

I do realize that one needs to think of the audience, too. As I write a screenplay, I can sense when the audience needs something funny to break the tension, sometimes.

And I appreciate how Ricky Gervais will not be on his deathbed, saying, "I did all that work. And I never expressed myself."

My point is: one of the best ways to nurture yourself is to truly express yourself.

Author Julia Cameron wrote that "original" means that you are the origin of the work.

You are the writer of your life. Your creativity can be expressed in how you listen to a distraught friend or how you juggle the details of your life. Realize that every human being is creative, not just the "artists."

Write your life for yourself and your joy will radiate to other people.

Now that is a kind, compassionate service to us all.

Some Thoughts on "How to Really Live Your Life"—and Strengthen Your Spirit

"What is life about for you?" Your answer will probably take the form of a "global metaphor." Such metaphors sound like "life is a test," "life is suffering and you can only hope for a reward in the afterlife." I have a couple of friends who subscribe to that last global metaphor. And guess what?—they experience a lot of suffering. A global metaphor (or label) colors every experience you have. Why? Your global metaphor influences your interpretations of what you experience in life. As I am writing this, I'm celebrating the release of one of my novels online. I wrote the first draft of this particular novel 28 years ago. And at this moment, I feel a mixture of joy, relief and some sadness. But I'm okay with all of the feelings because I look at life with my global metaphor of "Life is an adventure, a classroom, a theme park, and an opportunity for joy and personal growth."

In adventure stories, a hero will endure tough times and

bruises. But the adventure is worth it. Why? Because it's the way we get to feel fully alive. So I invite you to choose your global metaphor about life with care. And be sure to write your life for yourself. For example, I know some people who get caught up with just focusing on money. How sad. Not everything is about money. To find the true value of a past experience to you, ask yourself these questions:
- Did you have some fun?
- Did you learn anything?
- Did you express yourself?
- Did you express love to someone?
- Were you creative?

Be sure to really live your life.

* * * * * *

9) How You Can Turn Big Problems Into Big Successes

When was the last time someone really disappointed you? What happened?

When someone left me in a bad situation, I coined the phrase: "From Lemons to Lemonade to Lemon Meringue Pie." You can do better than survive a bad situation; you can come out on top! We'll use the N.O.W. process:

N – Note how to contain the damage
O – Open ways to make it better than your first imagining
W – Wrangle support

1. Note how to contain the damage

When someone you trust drops the ball and leaves you with a bad situation, it's time for you to contain the damage.

That is, make sure that no further damage occurs. For example, if you promise a client that a project will be done on Tuesday, Sept. 24th, and an important team member quits, you must find a way to avoid disappointing your own client. That is "containing the damage."

Turning lemons to lemonade is like "containing the damage." And it's no fun. But turning lemons to lemon meringue pie feels much better. Why? Because it feels like a progression:

- Lemons = bad situation
- Lemonade = it's better but it's still sour (containing the damage)
- Lemon Meringue Pie = Now it's sweet

For me, a lemon meringue pie is better than lemons. And this leads to our next step.

2. Open ways to make it better than your first imagining

A film composer used up four hours of my time tinkering with themes and orchestrations while I listened on the telephone. Then she quit, in favor of doing something else with her time. At that point, I didn't get four hours of my life back and I did not have any music for my film project. The schedule was thrown off, and I lost time I needed to devote to other projects I was leading.

In addition, I felt betrayed because I had worked with this person a number of times over the years. In response, I said, "This is a new chapter. You have not done this before. I could count on you before."

Some hours later, I thought: "How can I make this better than just putting a band-aid on it?" Soon some thoughts arose: "What if I write the melodies? That would be fun. And I'd expand my experience with music, both writing and producing music."

I managed to make things better than my first imagining.

Another time I made things better was from inside the tight confines of an MRI machine. If you have not been in an MRI machine, let me set the stage. You're placed on a moveable shelf and put into a wall with only an inch clearance over your nose. A number of people take valium to endure this.

I didn't take a pill. Instead, I closed my eyes and imagined how to do a flying scene for the feature film I was directing. I figured out how to do a flying scene for $200.00 instead of paying $9,000.00 (studio and equipment rentals). The finished scene looked great in the film.

3. Wrangle support

For you to have pie, you need to add something, the crust—or in this case, some support. Often to make things better, you'll find that getting help will improve the project. So when the film composer quit unexpectedly, I had a discussion with another film director about the elements needed for the film soundtrack music. And I sought the sound recording expertise of a music producer I know. [I talk about how to get support and how you can be unstoppable in my book *Nothing Can Stop You This Year: How to Unleash Your Hidden Power to Persuade Well, Get More Done, Gain Sudden Profits, Command Intuition and Feel Great*—free chapter at Amazon.com]

Remember the phrase: "From Lemons to Lemonade to Lemon Meringue Pie." It reminds us of a new pattern for dealing with a surprise problem. Take the "Lemons to Pie" phrase and use it as inspiration. Find out how you can go from controlling damage to making things better than your first imagining.

Some Thoughts on "How You Can Turn Big Problems Into Big Successes"—and Strengthen Your Spirit

What is life for? This is a spiritual question. I have a friend "Jonathan" who apparently lives for comfort. No romantic relationship for him: "Too much trouble." No pursuit of a job that utilizes his college degree: "To hard and too uncertain." Jonathan merely works at a job only because a friend needed some help. Jonathan likes "no problems." Okay. Everyone can choose his or her path.

Now I have a question. What if life was about being skillful with our problems and growing as people as we stretch to overcome problems? Author Brian Tracy emphasizes: "On your business card, no matter what your title is, belongs 'problem solver.'"

* * * * * *

10) Beware of Friends' Conventional Thinking: Your Success is on *Your* Path

Ever consider doing something unusual with your life, but your friends tried to dissuade you from pursuing new possibilities? We need to remember that when someone says, "It's not possible," they may be only talking about themselves. You need to decouple yourself from your friends' conventional thinking. We'll use the H.O.W. process:

H—Honor your heart's desire

O—Open your eyes to the unconventional

W—Wander through possibilities

1. Honor your heart's desire

When a friend says something is not possible for you to accomplish, what are they doing? Now that is a good question. Maybe they're trying to protect you from a big disappointment. But you can't avoid all disappointments. Disappointments pop up in life no matter what we're doing. But there is a bigger pain than disappointment. We feel more pain around "I could've tried that. I'll never know what good things may have happened if I only had the courage to try something new."

Start a new way of thinking. Don't just focus on how much money you can make. Start thinking of "units of life." Some things that we do create more positive energy. A poet may write poetry her whole life and make zero money from poetry. But I have a question. How much is her own smile worth? If you're her son, it's worth a lot. One because you love her and two because with her happiness in writing poetry, she is now rarely angry.

Now it's your turn. Answer these questions: What brings more positive energy to your life? What is an expression of your heart's desire?

2. Open your eyes to the unconventional

Let's look at some conventional things that a friend may say:

- *That won't make any money.*

How do they know? Numerous people thought that Disneyland would fail. Before that, several people called Walt Disney's first animated feature film *Snow White and the Seven Dwarfs* "Disney's folly." Well, they were wrong! *Snow White* was an instant hit on its first of many releases.

Think about it. From "Disney's Folly" to Walt Disney World and now a multi-billion dollar entertainment empire.

Thank goodness, Walt Disney had the guts to listen to his own heart and press beyond conventional thinking.

- *You'll be wasting your time.*

Again, how does the friend know? I was the lead singer of a rock band in the '80's. I take what I learned then to my recent studio sessions. Currently, I go into the recording studio to produce movie soundtrack music and music for my audio programs like *Be Heard and Be Trusted* and *Darkest Secrets of Persuasion and Seduction Masters: How to Protect Yourself and Turn the Power to Good* (You can listen to previews on iTunes.com). I was *not* wasting my time in the recording studio back in the '80's. I was learning so much about music. When I direct a film, I know how to communicate with a film music composer. You never know what past experience you can apply to your next project—or next phase of life.

- *Would you just concentrate on one thing?*

The current culture seems to celebrate specialists. But in the past, people who did more than one thing were called Renaissance people. They explored many fields. In college, I had a double major: psychology and television production. I'm still working in both fields with nonfiction books and feature films. And I truly enjoy the variety! It fires me up! I'm energized. I'm writing fiction and nonfiction each day. I bounce back and forth. What fun!

Here is the important point: *be sure to finish projects.* Because I finish projects, I'm one of the least frustrated artists I know. (For example, my children's graphic novel *Crystal Pegasus* is available at Amazon.com.)

- *I've never seen (a movie, a book, a song, etc.) like that before.*

Fine. If you have not seen it, it could be fresh. No one truly knows what the market will accept or cherish at a given moment. Author Greg Bear told me that it took ten years before the audience found one of his books. So be it. Stay in the game. Put yourself into your work. Honor your voice.

It is generally regarded that Marlon Brando brought a new realism with his style of acting in the 1950s. People complained: "He's mumbling." But others said, "He's so real!" Numerous actors were influenced by Marlon Brando: James Dean, Montgomery Cliff, Martin Sheen and more.

You may be starting something new and great.

3. Wander through possibilities

During one of my classes with my graduate students each semester, I draw on the whiteboard the trajectory of a number of people's careers. My illustration looks like a big squiggle as opposed to what people would prefer—a simple rising slope for the upward movement of their careers. There are times when we seem to be wandering off course. Then, I tell the students that my clients report that often an "off course time" provides needed experience and wisdom.

Everything you have done counts and can be used for the next level of your life.

Author Debra Fine tells about how she began as a shy, heavy-set child who was ostracized. So she became an engineer, in part, to have a career that avoided much socializing. Then, in search of additional funds, she came to teach a class that later served as inspiration for her book *The Fine Art of Small Talk*. She had no idea that a shy person (herself) would become an expert on socializing and networking.

Here's the important lesson. Welcome a bit of wandering through possibilities.

As author Joseph Campbell said, "We must be willing to relinquish the life we've planned, so as to have the life that is waiting for us."

Remember to move beyond your friends' conventional thinking.

They truly do not know your best path—that arises from your personal intuition.

Use these methods:

H—Honor your heart's desire

O—Open your eyes to the unconventional

W—Wander through possibilities

They work. I know. I've enjoyed so many unconventional opportunities.

Someone might describe my life as:
- from model to motivational speaker
- from karate instructor to communication coach
- from day camp teacher to rock band singer/keyboardist
- from graduate school instructor to motion picture director/actor/producer
- from shy kid to author of 22 books on Amazon.com [It takes courage to put your thoughts and feelings out there in the world. Trust me on this one.]

Some of my friends and family members *attempted to dissuade me from all of the above*. That's fine. It's not their life. I'm having a lot of fun with my own life.

How about you? What positive experiments in living do you want to try?

New opportunities are waiting to bloom for you—when you're somewhat unconventional.

Some Thoughts on "Beware of Friends' Conventional Thinking: Your Success is on YOUR Path"—and Strengthen Your Spirit

Numerous spiritual paths mention that we are meant to grow where we're planted. In other words, we're to fully express our potential. If you allow your friends' conventional thinking to choke your efforts, you might be allowing something truly bad to happen. When a human being is expressing herself creatively, she often feels elated. Don't deny the world the positive energy that it needs. Find your own path.

Conventional thinking is average thinking. And you're not here to be "just average." A number of researchers note that numerous individuals possess the potential to do great things. The problem is: many individuals have been conditioned to keep a lid on their own natural brilliance. Why? Usually some form of fear holds them back. Let's use a fictional story to look at this in another way.

George passes away. He's at the Pearly Gates and the "Angel on Duty" says, "So how did it go down there on Earth?"

"All right, I guess," George replies.

"All right? Just all right?! Don't you know that it was all provided? You had all you needed—the talent, skills, right connections—to have a joyful adventure of life."

"Really? I didn't know. Anyway, I had a problem," George says.

"What problem?"

"Fear."

"Oh! You missed it."

"What?"

"You were supposed to use fear as a hurdle that you would climb over and go higher in life," confirmed the

Angel on Duty.

So the fear of what other people would say is something we're supposed to get over.

We need to listen to our own heart and intuition. This is not just about having more fun. It's about having the spiritual journey that serves our highest good. People living their highest good naturally feel kind, compassionate and generous to those people who are near them.

Conclusion to Book IV:

We have covered 10 Topics related to strengthening your spirit. My goal with this section was to bring spirituality into daily life and to illuminate how our daily choices really reflect the spiritual path that we're on.

Now let's move forward to my *Final Word* of this book . . .

A FINAL WORD AND
THE SPRINGBOARD TO YOUR DREAMS

This book began as my response to the tragedy of my friend Joe's suicide. I hope that this book will help prevent other tragic outcomes.

We have explored details about Opportunists and Guilters. We uncovered the 10 Vulnerabilities to Spiritual Seduction and the Dark Seducer's Methods (Darkest Secrets of Spiritual Seduction Masters):

S—Submerge your self-esteem

E—Encourage self-loathing

D—Deny your intuition

U—Undermine your ability to hold two opposing thoughts

C—Comfort you with "friends"

E—Eliminate your support system

Further, we have experienced empowering quotes from Spiritual Leaders and those people momentarily gifted with nourishing ideas.

This book serves to begin the conversation.

As we come to the close of this book, I'm grateful to have had the opportunity to share insights with you.

To gain more value from this book, be sure to go through it and develop your own To Do List. Take some action. Any action towards improving skills and nurturing yourself is helpful. I often say, "Better than zero."

Please consider gaining special training through my coaching (phone and in-person), workshops, presentations and Top Five Group Elite Video Training.

As you continue to work toward enhancing your life, you are likely to come up against some tough situations. To be supportive I've written a number of books . . .

- Darkest Secrets of Charisma
- Darkest Secrets of Persuasion and Seduction Masters: How to Protect Yourself and Turn the Power to Good
- Darkest Secrets of Negotiation Masters
- Darkest Secrets of Making a Pitch to the Film and Television Industry
- Darkest Secrets of Film Directing
- Darkest Secrets of the Film and Television Industry Every Actor Should Know
- Darkest Secrets of Spiritual Seduction Masters
- Secrets of Awesome Dinner Guests: What Walt Disney, Steve Jobs, Oprah Winfrey, Albert Einstein, Martin Luther King, Jr., Helen Keller, and John Lasseter Can Teach You About Success and Fulfillment
- Success Secrets of Rich, Smart and Powerful People: How You Can Use Leverage for Business Success
  See my blog at www.BeHeardandBeTrusted.com

The best to you and may you continue to change the world,
Tom
Tom Marcoux,
America's Communication Coach, TFG Thought Leader
P.S. See **Free Chapters** of Tom Marcoux's 22 books at http://amzn.to/ZiCTRj
Titles include:
Be Heard and Be Trusted
Nothing Can Stop You This Year
Truth No One Will Tell You
10 Seconds to Wealth
Your Secret Charisma
Wake Up Your Spirit to Prosperity
The Cat Advantage
— and more.
(For coaching, reach Tom Marcoux at tomsupercoach@gmail.com)

EXCERPT FROM
DARKEST SECRETS OF PERSUASION AND SEDUCTION MASTERS: HOW TO PROTECT YOURSELF AND TURN THE POWER TO GOOD

by Tom Marcoux, America's Communication Coach

BOOK I
Darkest Secrets of Persuasion Masters

I never expected to write *Darkest Secrets of Persuasion and Seduction Masters: How to Protect Yourself and Turn the Power to Good.*

But I was angry and I had to stand up for you.

When I was a child, I was hurt badly. My parents could not protect me. As a young man, in one of my first business deals, I was hurt terribly.

Now, I am in my 40's, with gray in my hair, and for 27 years I have been taking action to protect people.

And now is the time for me to protect you with the Countermeasures I reveal in this book.

Every human being needs to be able to break the trance that a Manipulator creates. You need to make good decisions so you are safe and you keep growing—and you are not cut down and crippled.

This Darkest Secrets material is so intense that I first released it only with the counterbalance of my most energizing and uplifting books, Nothing Can Stop You This Year! and 10 Seconds to Wealth: Master the Moment Using Your Divine Gifts.

An interviewer asked me: "Who can be the Manipulator?"

A co-worker, a boss, a salesperson, someone you're dating, and someone you think is a friend.

Now is the time—this very minute—for me to write this book to protect you.

I must speak the truth.

These darkest secrets of "persuasion masters" are …

Wait a minute! Let's say it plainly: These are the darkest secrets of masters of manipulation. Throughout this book, I will call these people what they are: Manipulators.

Dictionary.com defines "manipulate" as "To influence or manage shrewdly or deviously…. To tamper with or falsify for personal gain."

In this book, we will look on a manipulator as one who

deviously influences someone with no concern about that person's well-being, and who causes harm to that person.

Here is the first Darkest Secret:

Darkest Secret #1:
Manipulators Make You Hurt
and Then Offer the Salve.

Manipulators would invite you to go out in the sun for hours and then sell you the salve to soothe your burns. The problem is that we don't notice that this is what they're doing.

For example, you're considering the purchase of a house. A Manipulator asks the question, "So, where would you put your TV?" This question is designed to put you into a trance.

Dictionary.com defines "trance" as "a half-conscious state, seemingly between sleeping and waking, in which ability to function voluntarily may be suspended." Let's condense this: in a trance you may not be able to function freely.

Here is the second Darkest Secret:

Darkest Secret #2:
Manipulators Put You into a Trance.

To protect yourself, you must learn to use Countermeasures to Break the Trance.

All the Countermeasures (actions you can take to break the trance) in this book will make you stronger and more capable of protecting yourself.

Now, we'll view the third Darkest Secret:

Darkest Secret #3:
Manipulators Care Nothing for You and Human Decency: They'll lie, cheat, and do whatever they need to do so they win—but their charm masks all this.

Let's return to the example of a Manipulator selling you a house. A Manipulator does not pause for an instant to see if you can truly afford the new house. The Manipulator would neglect to mention that you will not only have your mortgage payment of $900. There will be additional costs: home repairs, property tax, water, electricity, homeowner's insurance, and more. The Manipulator only emphasizes what he or she knows you want to hear: "Look! $900 is better than the $1500 you're paying for rent, which is just going down the toilet. And the $900 is an investment."

Let's go back to **Darkest Secret #1:**
Manipulators make you hurt and then offer the salve.

The Manipulator has you feeling good about the solution (salve) and feeling bad about your current life situation.

How? A Manipulator will make you hurt through questions such as:

- What bothers you about paying $1500 a month for rent? (The Manipulator will use a derisive tone when he says the word rent.)
- What is not smart about paying rent on someone else's house instead of investing in your own house?
- How do you feel about your children walking in the neighborhood where you live now?

Do you see how these questions are designed to make you

hurt enough so that you'll buy?

An interviewer asked me, "Tom, aren't these good arguments for purchasing a house?"

"What we're looking at is the intention of the influencer," I replied. "Let's look at our definition of a manipulator as one who deviously influences someone with no concern about that person's well-being, and who causes harm to that person. If the person truly cannot afford the house, he or she will be harmed by buying it. If the manipulator conceals the truth, the manipulator is doing harm. That's the important difference."

Some friends of mine are ethical and helpful real estate agents who truthfully reveal the whole situation and help the purchaser achieve her own goals.

In this book, we are talking about another type of person; that is, unethical Manipulators.

* * *

In any given moment, we need to remember the tactics Manipulators use. We will focus on the word D.A.R.K. so you can remember details easily and protect yourself from Manipulators.

D — Dangle something for nothing
A — Alert to scarcity
R — Reveal the Desperate Hot Button
K — Keep on pushing buttons

We'll begin with *Dangle something for nothing* with the next chapter.

CHAPTER TWO: DANGLE SOMETHING FOR NOTHING

The first method of D.A.R.K. is *Dangle Something for Nothing.*

What do conmen and conwomen do to seize your attention? They make you think you're getting a "steal."

I recently saw a documentary in which a conman on a street in England showed a toy that looked like it was dancing. This fake product was actually dancing because of a hidden, invisible thread. The conman was dangling something for nothing. The Entranced Buyer thought he was getting something worth $20 for only $5. That was the trick. The Entranced Buyer felt that he was getting $15 extra of value for his $5. What the Buyer really got was something worth nothing. Similarly, I know someone who purchased a copy of a Disney movie from a street vendor in San Francisco. She brought the copy home and it was unwatchable—and the street vendor was never seen again.

An old phrase goes, "A conman cannot con someone who is not looking for something for nothing."

How to Protect Yourself from "Dangle Something for Nothing"

Stop! Get on your cell phone and talk through the "deal" with someone you know who thinks clearly. Go home. Think about it. Do some research on the Internet. Listen to your gut feelings. If the salesman or conman is too insistent, get away from that Manipulator. Get quiet. Have a cup of water. Cool down. Break the Trance!

Break the Trance and Identify the Crucial Detail

Earlier, I mentioned that a Manipulator puts you into a trance. An added problem is that we put ourselves into a trance. For example, as you read this, are you thinking about your right toe? Most likely not (unless you stubbed your toe recently). The point is that we only focus on a tiny percentage of what is going on in our life.

Around fifteen years ago, I caused myself trouble because I put myself into a trance. I discovered that under certain conditions, friendship can make you nearly deaf. Here's how: I was producing a song for a motion picture. A good friend was singing backup in the chorus. Because of our friendship, I wanted him to sound great. I completely missed the Crucial Detail. In this kind of situation, the Crucial Detail is that what truly counts is how the lead singer sounds! I made a song that I could not release. What a waste of time and money! I had put myself into a trance.

In any situation in which the Manipulator is "dangling something for nothing," we often fall into a trance and miss the Crucial Detail. The most important detail is not that we're saving money if we order before midnight tonight. What counts is whether the product creates a lasting, crucial benefit in our lives. And is the benefit of the product worth the cost? Some people even program themselves to make mistakes by saying, "I can't pass up a bargain." The bargain is not the Crucial Detail.

Secrets to Break the Trance

This is the process of B.R.E.A.K.S. It will help you remember the proven methods to break a trance.

B — Breathe
R — Relax

E — Envision
A — Act on aromas
K — Keep moving
S — Smile

Secret #1: Breathe

Remember Darkest Secret #1: Manipulators make you hurt and then offer the salve. The Manipulator wants to put you into a state of being that fills you with a sense of urgency and anxiety. Oh, no! I'm going to miss the sale!

Stop this highly vulnerable state. Take a deep breath. Do it now. Take a deep breath and let your belly "get fat" by filling it with air. As you breathe out, let your belly deflate. Breathe in through your nose and breathe out through your mouth. This is called belly-breathing. Repeat the actions of belly-breathing three times. Good. Now, do you feel different? Remember, when you are relaxed, you are strong.

Secret #2: Relax

You become stronger when you condition yourself to relax in the face of adversity. Researchers note that when an Olympic athlete is confronted with the most stressful moment in her life, she has prepared in advance. She has given herself ways to calm down. Two powerful methods are described in this section about B.R.E.A.K.S. One is breathing, and the other is envisioning.

A special part of relaxing is the effective use of your posture. Many of us think that we're relaxed when we slouch. However, I was taught by three physical therapists that when you sit up and align your vertebrae, you are more relaxed because your back's bone structure is naturally supporting you. Many of us discover that placing a pillow behind the lumbar-area of our back helps us sit up better. If you are sitting or standing when talking with a Manipulator, ensure that your posture is aligned. You will have more power to protect yourself.

Secret #3: Envision

Envision an image that makes you feel strong. Often, our strongest images come from movies that we saw when we were young. Some of my clients envision being strong like Xena the Warrior Princess or Superman. One client thinks of Sean Connery as James Bond. Immediately, this client walks smoothly with poise. He feels confident. Act as if you are, and you are!

Also, envision yourself being quite aware of your surroundings. On vacation, many of us become entranced by our new surroundings. Travelers let their guard down. A conperson catches them at a weak moment. It's important to stay in the present and be alert to what's going on. Stay present with your needs, and shop around before making a large purchase. Be prepared to walk away.

Watch out for Manipulators who are slick, fast talkers. They try to get your money, and just minutes after they succeed, you realize what happened.

But this is *not* for you! You can remind yourself with an internal comment: "I am aware. What is really going on here?"

Secret #4: Act on Aromas

Let's notice the power of an aroma.

Smell is a potent wizard that transports you
across thousands of miles
and all the years you have lived.
– Helen Keller

*Nothing is more memorable than a smell.
One scent can be unexpected, momentary and fleeting,
yet conjure up a childhood summer
beside a lake in the mountains.
– Diane Ackerman*

You need to be able to calm down within seconds. One of the fastest ways to do that is to use a favorite aroma. One of my clients has conditioned herself to calm down by smelling lavender. The process for her was to recline in a hot bath and smell lavender simultaneously. Now, the smell of lavender relaxes her limbs quickly.

Remember, when you are relaxed, you neutralize the Manipulator's tactic to make you feel that buying something now is an urgent matter. You let go of any anxious feelings the Manipulator seeks to create in you. Use an aroma to help you feel relaxed and strong.

Secret #5: Keep Moving

A trance often transfixes or freezes us, making us still. Sometimes, the most powerful way to break a trance is to use a movement that you prepared in advance. One of my clients closes his right fist and taps it on his right thigh. In his mind, he repeats the phrase: "I am my own person!" This helps him break out of a trance induced by a Manipulator.

Another client quietly snaps her fingers near her waist. This reminds her to "snap out of it."

Secret #6: Smile

Smile when you detect a Manipulator using a manipulation method. Why? If you get angry, you become vulnerable. Remember: Manipulators make you hurt and then offer the salve.

Often when we're angry, we don't realize that beneath the anger is fear. What fear? Fear of being taken advantage of. Become strong when you identify what makes you angry.

Pull out a sheet of paper or write in your personal journal. Write the headings of two columns.

a) What Makes Me Angry
b) What Fear Might Underlie My Anger

Write the two items next to each other.
Here is an example:
A clerk is rude to me. ===> I'm afraid that I'm worthless and not worthy of being treated with respect and kindness

The list above provides good information for you. When confronted with a Manipulator that pushes your fear buttons, you can say to yourself, "Oh! That touched my fear of losing an advantage. Okay, I feel this fear—but I am more than this fear. I am intelligent and capable."

You will feel better when you smile upon detecting a Manipulator's tactic. You will feel more in control. Researchers have shown that the act of smiling actually changes one's body chemistry. Get your body on your side.

Smile and break the trance-of-anxiety that the Manipulator attempts to use against you.

Point to Remember:
Manipulators dangle something for nothing.

Your Countermeasure:
Identify the Crucial Detail. Use these questions and statements:

- What benefit do I really want?
- Is this benefit worth the costs?
- Do I know all the costs?
- I will ask and ask until I am certain about the risks involved.
- Finally, I will contact someone I respect who is outside the area and run the situation past this trusted advisor.

End of Excerpt from
Darkest Secrets of Persuasion and Seduction Masters: How to Protect Yourself and Turn the Power to Good
Copyright 2013 Tom Marcoux Media, LLC

Purchase your copy of this book (paperback or ebook) at Amazon.com or BarnesandNoble.com
See **Free Chapters** of Tom Marcoux's 22 books at http://amzn.to/ZiCTRj

* * * * * *

PARTIAL LIST OF REFERENCES for *Darkest Secrets of Spiritual Seduction Masters*

*1 - Study noted on page 237-238 of *Nerve: Poise Under Pressure , Serenity Under Stress, and the Brave New Science of Fear and Cool* by Taylor Clark.

*2 - from a study noted on page 226 of *The Stress Eating Cure* by Dr. Rachael F. Heller and Dr. Richard F. Heller

*3 - from *How to Love: Choosing Well at Every Stage of Life* by Gordon Livingston, M.D.

*4, *5 - from page 184 of *Nudge: Improving Decisions About Health, Wealth and Happiness* by Richard H. Thaler and Cass R. Sunstein

*6 - from page 141 of *Health Psychology: An Introduction to Behavior and Health* by Linda Brannon and Jess Feist

*7 - Abundant evidence that severe and acute emotional stress following an earthquake or other natural disaster or the loss of a loved one can result in hypertension, a heart attack or sudden death . . . noted in Rosch, P. J. (1994a) Does Stress Cause Hypertension? Stress Medicine, 10:141-143. and Rosch, P. J. (1994b) Can Stress Cause Coronary Heart Disease? Stress Medicine, 10:207-210

ABOUT THE AUTHOR

Tom Marcoux helps people like you fulfill big dreams. Known as America's Communication Coach and TFG Thought Leader, Tom has authored 22 books with sales in 15 countries. One of his *Darkest Secrets* books rose to #1 on Amazon.com Hot New Releases in Business Life (and in Business Communication). He guides clients and audiences (IBM, Sun Microsystems, etc.) to success in job interviewing, public speaking, media relations, and branding. A member of the National Speakers Association, he is a professional coach and guest expert on TV, radio, and print, and was dubbed "the Personal Branding Instructor" by the *San Francisco Examiner*. Tom addressed National Association of Broadcasters' Conference six years running. With a degree in psychology, Tom has served as a guest lecturer at **Stanford University**, DeAnza, & California State University, and teaches public speaking, science fiction cinema/literature, Designing Careers, and comparative religion at Academy of Art University. Winner of a special award at the **Emmys**, Tom wrote, directed, and produced a feature film that the distributor took to the **Cannes film market**, and the film gained international distribution. He is engaged in book/film projects *Crystal Pegasus* (children's) and *TimePulse* (science fiction). See TomSuperCoach.com and Tom's well-received blog at www.BeHeardandBeTrusted.com

Tom Marcoux can help you with **speech writing** and **coaching for your best performance.**
As Tom says, *Make Your Speech a Pleasant Beach.*
Join Tom's Linkedin.com group: *Executive Public Speaking and Communication Power.*
Get a **Free** report: "9 Deadly Mistakes to Avoid for Your

Next Speech and 9 Surefire Methods" at
http://tomsupercoach.com/freereport9Mistakes4Speech.html

Tom Marcoux has trained CEOs, small business owners, and graduate students to speak with impact and gain audiences' tremendous approval and cooperation. *Learn how to present and get thunderous applause!*

"Tom, Thanks for your coaching and work with me on revising my speech at a major university. Working with you has been so enlightening for me. Through your gentle prodding and guidance I was able to write a speech that connects with the audience. I wish everyone could experience the transformation I have undergone. You have helped me discover the warm and compelling stories that now make my speech reach hearts and uplift minds. This was truly an empowering experience. I cannot thank you enough for your great assistance." — J.S.

Become a fan of Tom's graphic novels/feature films:
Science fiction: *TimePulse*
www.facebook.com/timepulsegraphicnovel

Fantasy Thriller: *Jack AngelSword*
type "JackAngelSword" at Facebook.com

Children's Fantasy: *Crystal Pegasus*
www.facebook.com/crystalpegasusandrose

See **Free Chapters** of Tom Marcoux's 22 books at http://amzn.to/ZiCTRj

Special Offer Just for Readers of this Book:

Contact Tom Marcoux at tomsupercoach@gmail.com for special discounts on books, coaching, workshops and presentations. Just mention your experience with this book.

www.ingramcontent.com/pod-product-compliance
Lightning Source LLC
Chambersburg PA
CBHW071311110426
42743CB00042B/1254